100 Quick Quizzes

100 Quick Quizzes

Camilla de la Bedoyere

Miles Kelly

First published in 2010 as *Flip Quiz: General Knowledge Ages 9–10* by Miles Kelly Publishing Ltd
Harding's Barn, Bardfield End Green, Thaxted, Essex, CM6 3PX, UK

This edition published in 2013

2 4 6 8 10 9 7 5 3 1

Publishing Director Belinda Gallagher
Creative Director Jo Cowan
Assistant Editor Claire Philip
Cover Designer Jo Cowan
Designers Jo Cowan, Joe Jones
Junior Designer Kayleigh Allen
Image Manager Liberty Newton
Production Manager Elizabeth Collins
Reprographics Stephan Davis, Jennifer Hunt, Thom Allaway

ISBN 978-1-78209-125-7

Printed in China

British Library Cataloguing-in-Publication Data
A catalogue record for this book is available from the British Library

The publisher would like to thank the following sources for the use of their photographs:

COVER
Dreamstime.com Quiz 12 Mar...) Ferdericb; 39 (2) Aprescindere ,
(4) Ggw1962, (8) Irina Iglin... rayanan; 53 Jakub Cejpek;
60 (5) Bcnewell, (6) Stephen Jam... Tupinamba, (4) Hugo Rosseels;
72 Sean Gladwell; 75 Stuart Pearce... Fernandes; 86 Bambi L. Dingman;
88 Kaspri; 94 Braendan Yong; ... 50 section bars Perseomedusa
Fotolia.com Quiz 7 Maksym Gor... atyan, (9) EcoView; 14 robynmac;
18 Monkey Business; 19 (5) Elen... 21 Antony McAula; 25 Maksim
Shebeko; 31 get4art; 35 linou... orr; 49 (1) Stephen Coburn,
(2) Melisback, (4) TRITOOTH, (...) DannyBayne, (8), (9) Forgiss;
60 (3), (7) Lance Bellers; 70 (3) ... pu; 96; 100 (4) Uros Petrovic,
(5) Hubert Isselée, (9) Elena ... iio Perbellini, (10) fmg1308;
13 ZoneCreative; 30 (10) Tom W... M; 45 Pat Bonish; 50 (1) Stepan
Popov, (5) Laura Clay-... ns; 84 David Schliepp
Movie Store Collection Qui... . KG, Warner Bros. Pictures

All other photographs are from: digitalSTOCK, digitalvision, John Foxx, PhotoAlto, PhotoDisc, PhotoEssentials, PhotoPro, Stockbyte
All artwork from the Miles Kelly Artwork Bank

Every effort has been made to acknowledge the source and copyright holder of each picture.
Miles Kelly Publishing apologises for any unintentional errors or omissions.

Made with paper from a sustainable forest

www.mileskelly.net   info@mileskelly.net

www.factsforprojects.com

CONTENTS

How to play
Read these pages before you start

Living World • Quizzes 1–10
All about animals and plants

Healthy Living • Quizzes 11–20
About your body and keeping fit and well

Wonderful Words • Quizzes 21–30
This section will test your knowledge of English

Super Science • Quizzes 31–40
A great section for budding scientists

Number Crunchers • Quizzes 41–50
Good at maths? Then you'll love this section

Our World • Quizzes 51–60
All about the wonderful world we live in

Past Times • Quizzes 61–70
This will test your knowledge of history

How We Live • Quizzes 71–80
A fun section about people around the world

True or False • Quizzes 81–90
A quick-fire section about lots of different topics

Lucky Dip • Quizzes 91–100
A mixed bag with lots of different subjects – great fun!

Scorecards
Ten scorecards to record your results

HOW TO PLAY

To start

Choose which section you want to play. There are 10 sections, 10 quizzes per section and 10 questions per quiz.

Player/team 1 will always play odd-numbered quizzes – 1, 3, 5, 7 and 9.
Player/team 2 will always play even-numbered quizzes – 2, 4, 6, 8 and 10.

Question & Answer quizzes

Quiz number
There are ten quizzes in each section.

Questions
There are ten questions per quiz.

Illustrated fact
Learn a new fact to amaze your friends.

Flash symbol
This symbol means that the opposite quiz has a Picture clue to help you to answer.

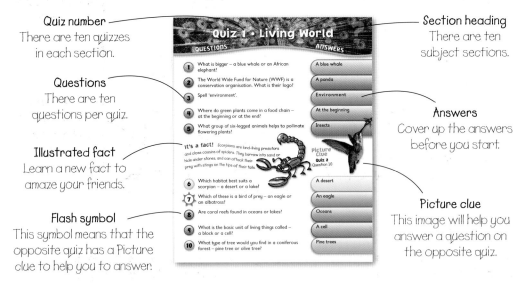

Section heading
There are ten subject sections.

Answers
Cover up the answers before you start.

Picture clue
This image will help you answer a question on the opposite quiz.

Playing on your own

Cover up the answers before you start. You will play all eight Question & Answer quizzes and fill in your scorecard.

Playing with a friend or in teams

See how Claire and Simon play to help you with your game.

1. Simon covers up Quiz 2 so Claire can't see it while she asks him questions on Quiz 1.
2. Claire asks Simon Questions 1–10 of Quiz 1.
3. For each correct answer, Claire adds a tick to his scorecard. For each incorrect answer, Claire leaves the space blank.
4. Simon asks Claire Questions 1–10 of Quiz 2.
5. Simon fills in Claire's scorecard.
6. Once they have answered all ten questions each, they add up the final score to see who wins that game.

Picture Challenge quizzes

Playing on your own

Cover up the answers before you start. You will play both Picture Challenge quizzes and fill in your scorecard.

Playing with a friend

Claire and Simon reach the last two quizzes in the section, 9 and 10.

1. They cover up the answers before they start.
2. Claire shows Simon the pictures for Quiz 9.
2. Simon writes down his answers on a piece of paper.
3. Claire checks Simon's answers to see how many he has got right and gives him a tick for each correct answer.
4. Then it's Simon's turn to challenge Claire. She will complete Quiz 10.

Question
There's one question for each Picture challenge.

Answers
Cover up the answers before you start.

Scorecards

Photocopy the scorecards instead of writing in the book, so you can play again and again. Don't forget – for each section, you'll need one scorecard for each player.

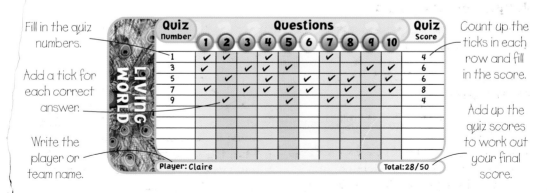

Fill in the quiz numbers.

Add a tick for each correct answer.

Write the player or team name.

Count up the ticks in each row and fill in the score.

Add up the quiz scores to work out your final score.

Quiz 1 • Living World

1 What is bigger – a blue whale or an African elephant?

A blue whale

2 The World Wide Fund for Nature (WWF) is a conservation organisation. What is their logo?

A panda

3 Spell 'environment'.

Environment

4 Where do green plants come in a food chain – at the beginning or at the end?

At the beginning

5 What group of six-legged animals helps to pollinate flowering plants?

Insects

It's a fact! Scorpions are land-living predators and close cousins of spiders. They burrow into sand or hide under stones, and can attack their prey with stings on the tips of their tails.

Picture Clue
Quiz 2
Question 10

6 Which habitat best suits a scorpion – a desert or a lake?

A desert

7 Which of these is a bird of prey – an eagle or an albatross?

An eagle

8 Are coral reefs found in oceans or lakes?

Oceans

9 What is the basic unit of living things called – a block or a cell?

A cell

10 What type of tree would you find in a coniferous forest – pine tree or olive tree?

Pine trees

Quiz 2 • Living World

1 What do fish use to breathe underwater?

Gills

2 Does 'excretion' mean getting rid of waste products from the body or hiding from predators?

Getting rid of waste products

3 What is an earthworm's habitat?

Soil

4 Do omnivores eat lots of different types of food including animals and plants, or just one type of food?

Lots of different types

5 What name is given to the tough outer covering of a tree trunk?

Bark

It's a fact! Most bears are omnivores and eat fruit, seeds, roots, insects and other animals. Pandas, however, eat mainly bamboo – a type of tough, tall-growing grass.

Picture Clue
Quiz 1
Question 7

6 Do leaves move towards sunlight, or away from it?

Towards sunlight

7 What R describes a large group of breeding penguins?

Rookery

8 What type of animals usually have fur or hair and feed their young with milk?

Mammals

9 Do butterflies prefer to fly at night or during the day?

During the day

10 Which bird lays the smallest eggs – birds of paradise or hummingbirds?

Hummingbirds

Quiz 3 • Living World

1 Which trees lose their leaves in autumn – evergreen or deciduous?

Deciduous

2 Do starfish live in marine or freshwater habitats?

Marine

3 All animals eat – are they called consumers or producers?

Consumers

4 Can plants be carnivores?

Yes, some plants trap and digest insects

5 Do plants that prefer damp conditions grow on a sand dune or in a swamp?

In a swamp

It's a fact! Stag beetles are becoming rare but you can help them survive by leaving wood to rot in the garden. Young beetles live and feed on the wood for up to six years before they mature.

Picture Clue
Quiz 4
Question 2

6 Would you find a stigma, style and ovary in the male or female part of a flower?

Female

7 Does a duck-billed platypus have fur?

Yes

8 What is the largest beetle – the stag beetle or the rhinoceros beetle?

Rhinoceros beetle

9 What is a butterfly larva better known as?

A caterpillar

10 How many eggs can a female cockroach lay in her life – 100 or 1000?

1000

Quiz 4 • Living World

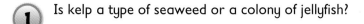
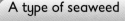
1 Is kelp a type of seaweed or a colony of jellyfish?

> A type of seaweed

2 Which large flightless bird lived on the island of Mauritius before becoming extinct?

> Dodo

3 What term describes animals that feed on the remains of dead creatures?

> Scavengers

4 What is the fleshy part of a plant that contains seeds?

> Fruit

5 Do birds know how to build nests by instinct, or do their parents teach them?

> They know by instinct

It's a fact! Mushrooms are a type of fungus. Most fungi feed on dead organisms, although some can feed on living things.

Picture Clue
Quiz 3
Question 9

6 What word describes animals that are coloured, or patterned, to blend in with their surroundings?

> Camouflaged

7 What type of duck has a green head – a shelduck or a mallard?

> A mallard

8 What is the name for the insect sense organs that grow on stalks?

> Antennae

9 Do mushrooms use sunlight to make their food by photosynthesis?

> No, they get food from dead organisms

10 Why are ladybirds brightly coloured?

> To warn predators that they taste bad

Quiz 5 • Living World

1 What is the control centre of a cell called – a nucleus or a nuclear?

A nucleus

2 Which of these foods are good sources of protein – eggs, bread, tuna, pasta?

Eggs and tuna

3 What O describes anything that is living?

Organism

4 What provides the energy that plants use to make their own food?

The Sun

5 What do dung beetles feed on?

Animal dung (poo or faeces)

It's a fact! Woolly mammoths lived during the Ice Age. They probably became extinct because the Earth got much warmer and humans hunted them for food.

Picture Clue
Quiz 6
Question 8

6 Do flamingos get their pink colouring from the water they wash in, or from the food they eat?

From the food they eat

7 In which part of your body would you find a lens?

Your eyes

8 Did woolly mammoths die out around four million years ago or 4000 years ago?

4000 years ago

9 What are the plants at the beginning of a food chain called – producers or creators?

Producers

10 Does a snake have more ribs than a blue whale?

Yes

Quiz 6 • Living World

QUESTIONS

ANSWERS

1 What L is another word for arms, legs or wings?

Limbs

2 Do all snakes lay eggs?

No, some give birth to live young

3 Mammals, birds, reptiles, amphibians, …? What is the fifth animal group?

Fish

4 Are bats blind?

No

5 During digestion, what does your body break down?

Food

It's a fact! Sea snakes are poisonous reptiles that spend most of their lives in water. Some give birth to live young at sea. Others come to land to lay their eggs.

Picture Clue
Quiz 5
Question 4

6 Are moulds living organisms?

Yes

7 Are kangaroos, koalas and wallabies types of marsupial or reptile?

Types of marsupial

8 Is a pumpkin a vegetable or a fruit?

A fruit (it contains seeds)

9 Which F is when male and female sex cells join to start a new living thing?

Fertilization

10 When did the dinosaurs die out – 6500 years ago or 65 million years ago?

65 million years ago

Quiz 7 • Living World

1 What piece of equipment might you use to look at something that is very small?

Microscope or magnifying glass

2 Lice, ticks and fleas are examples of parasites. Do they find their own food?

No, they live off food supplied by their host

3 What is the green chemical found in leaves – chlorine or chlorophyll?

Chlorophyll

4 What C is the female part of a plant?

Carpel

5 What runs fastest – a rhino or an ostrich?

An ostrich

It's a fact! When trees respire they use carbon dioxide and release oxygen – the gas we breathe. Trees in 10,000 square metres of woodland produce enough oxygen for just 45 people every year.

Picture Clue
Quiz 8
Question 9

6 Is a toadstool a type of fungus or a type of algae?

Fungus

7 What do vertebrates have that non-vertebrates lack?

A backbone or spine

8 Pterosaurs lived at the same time as the dinosaurs. Were they flying reptiles or swimming mammals?

Flying reptiles

9 What describes the way seeds move away from the parent plant – dispersal or disturbance?

Dispersal

10 What gas do trees release into the air?

Oxygen

Quiz 8 • Living World

1 Plants need water and sunlight to photosynthesise – what is the third thing they need to make food?

Carbon dioxide

2 Do herbivores feed on producers or other consumers?

Producers

3 What G is when a seed begins to grow?

Germination

4 Do hippos prefer wet or dry habitats?

Wet habitats

5 Which type of big cat is most endangered – leopard or tiger?

Tiger

It's a fact! Hippos have sensitive skin that dries out easily in the heat, so they wallow in water and mud to keep damp and cool. Mud-covered skin also prevents insects from biting.

Picture Clue
Quiz 7 Question 1

6 I am a type of green fruit and also a bird that lives in New Zealand. What am I?

A kiwi

7 What are a mushroom's seeds called – splits or spores?

Spores

8 What word describes an animal that is killed by another for food?

Prey

9 Which white-berried plant is hung in houses at Christmas time to encourage people to kiss?

Mistletoe

10 What V is another word for poison produced by some animals, such as snakes?

Venom

Quiz 9 • Living World

Meat or Veg?

Look at these animals. For each one,
say if it is a carnivore (meat eater),
a herbivore (plant eater) or an
omnivore (eats both meat and plants).

Quiz 10 • Living World

Animal Groups

What groups do these animals belong to?

Are they mammals, birds, reptiles, amphibians or fish?

Quiz 11 • Healthy Living

1 How many pairs of ribs do you have?

12

2 If I only eat vegetables, fruits and fish, am I a vegetarian?

No, fish is not a vegetable

3 Are the very tiny living things that can cause diseases called micro-organisms or mini-organisms?

Micro-organisms

4 What word is used to describe something you can eat – edible or eatable?

Edible

5 What are children's first teeth called?

Milk teeth

It's a fact! We sweat when we're hot, but also when we're scared or embarrassed. The whole body sweats, but the forehead, armpits, palms and soles of the feet are the sweatiest spots.

Picture Clue
Quiz 12
Question 3

6 My pupil lets light in, which helps me work out where things are and what they look like. What am I?

An eye

7 Where did yoga come from originally – Ireland or India?

India

8 What helps our bodies to cool down when we're very hot?

Sweat

9 When we exercise do we breathe quickly or slowly?

Quickly

10 What type of cooking pot is used to cook Chinese food?

A wok

Quiz 12 • Healthy Living

QUESTIONS

1 Does water contain fat?

2 What year will the Olympic Games be held in Rio de Janeiro, Brazil – 2014 or 2016?

3 Which of these is not a type of tooth – wolf fang, rhino horn, human incisor or elephant tusk?

4 Does food last longer in the freezer or the fridge?

5 Are all bacteria harmful?

It's a fact! Playing tennis burns up lots of energy. Men can burn up to 600 calories in a single match, and women up to 400 calories.

6 What gas is added to drinks to make them fizzy – oxygen or carbon dioxide?

7 Do bees make maple syrup?

8 How long is the intestine of a human adult – about 70 centimetres or about 7 metres?

9 Can you live with just one of your two kidneys?

10 What should you put on your skin to stop it burning in the Sun?

ANSWERS

No

2016

Rhino horn

The freezer

No

Picture Clue
QUIZ 11
Question 10

Carbon dioxide

No, bees make honey

About 7 metres

Yes

Sun block, or sun cream

Quiz 13 • Healthy Living

QUESTIONS

ANSWERS

1 Does your body need more or less oxygen when you're sleeping?

Less

2 Does eating tuna provide your body with protein or carbohydrate?

Protein

3 Which of these things is not edible: sushi, salami or tsunami?

Tsunami – it is a huge wave

4 Which sport uses a sword – karate, archery or fencing?

Fencing

5 Why is it good to eat oranges and blackcurrants when you are getting a cold?

They contain vitamin C, which helps fight colds

It's a fact! Tuna are large fish that can swim up to 70 kilometres an hour. Some types of tuna, such as the bluefin, are threatened by overfishing and are now protected by law.

Picture Clue
Quiz 14
Question 8

6 Are all animals pregnant for nine months, like humans?

No

7 How many bones are in the human body – 206 or 106?

206

8 What might a doctor use a scalpel for – to listen to your heart or to cut your skin?

To cut your skin (during an operation)

9 What G is another word for a disease-causing micro-organism?

Germ

10 Which of these is high in fat – nuts, bread or fruit juice?

Nuts

Quiz 14 • Healthy Living

1 Does your temperature go up or down when you have a fever?

Up

2 I am a fungus and I'm still alive when people use me to make bread rise. What am I?

Yeast

3 Can the palm of your hand sweat?

Yes

4 How long does a broken bone usually take to heal — six weeks or six months?

Six weeks

5 Which is not a seafood: prawns, mussels, squid or ham?

Ham — it comes from a pig

It's a fact! Yeast is also used to brew beer. Brewers used to throw away the leftover yeast, but since the early 1900s, the Marmite company has been boiling it down and selling it as a spread.

Picture Clue
Quiz 13
Question 4

6 Which C is a mineral found in milk that keeps bones strong?

Calcium

7 Do teeth have roots?

Yes

8 What is the big muscle in your mouth that helps to mix foods?

Tongue

9 What are the compartments of the heart called — chambers or cabins?

Chambers

10 If a mother has triplets, how many babies does she have?

Three

Quiz 15 • Healthy Living

1 Where would you find fluoride – in toothpaste or shampoo?

Toothpaste

2 Where would you find your molars – in your mouth or on your hands?

In your mouth – they are teeth

3 When diving, why do scuba divers carry tanks of oxygen on their backs?

So they can breathe underwater

4 Which has more oxygen – the air that we breathe out or the air that we breathe in?

The air that we breathe in

5 What is another word for finger or toe – joint or digit?

Digit

It's a fact! As well as wearing fins, masks and the Self Contained Underwater Breathing Apparatus (SCUBA), most divers wear wetsuits to keep them warm.

Picture Clue
Quiz 16
Question 1

6 I am your body's biggest organ and I cover you from head to toe. What am I?

Skin

7 Do viruses cause diseases or do they help to fight them?

They cause diseases

8 Is yoghurt a dairy food or a carbohydrate?

Dairy food

9 Which is likely to contain more germs when you buy it – uncooked meat or uncooked vegetables?

Uncooked meat

10 What does a doctor measure to find out how fast someone's heart is beating?

The pulse

Quiz 16 • Healthy Living

1 Which food comes from Italy and is made from flour, water and eggs?

Pasta

2 What might you get if your new shoes rub?

Blisters

3 What is your skeleton made up of?

Bones

4 What makes your body move – tendons or muscles?

Muscles

5 Which gas do muscles need to work – oxygen or carbon dioxide?

Oxygen

It's a fact! Almost half your body's weight is made up of muscles. Without muscles you wouldn't be able to move – even smiling uses the muscles in your face!

Picture Clue
Quiz 15
Question 1

6 What is the watery liquid in your mouth that helps to digest food called?

Saliva

7 Which animal eats another of its own kind – a cannibal or a carnivore?

A cannibal

8 Where does a baby grow inside its mother – in her womb or in her stomach?

In her womb

9 What keeps blood flowing in the right direction in your heart – valves or plugs?

Valves

10 What do you add to boiled milk to make yoghurt – butter or bacteria?

Bacteria

Quiz 17 • Healthy Living

1 What name is given to the bony case that protects your brain?

Skull

2 What will help to stop the spread of a cold – coughing into a tissue or cooking food thoroughly?

Coughing into a tissue

3 What do antibiotics kill?

Bacteria that can cause illness

4 What type of food is an avocado?

Fruit

5 Is butter made from vegetable oil or milk?

Milk

It's a fact! Dogs developed large canine teeth to hold their prey firmly so they could tear it apart. Rabbits don't need to do this because the vegetables they eat don't struggle!

Picture Clue
Quiz 18
Question 9

6 How many ribs do you have – 12 or 24?

24

7 Do arteries carry blood from muscles to the heart and lungs, or from the heart and lungs to muscles?

From the heart and lungs to muscles

8 Which animals have bigger canine teeth – rabbits or dogs?

Dogs

9 What is found in the middle of your leg and makes it bend?

Your knee

10 What liquid carries oxygen around your body?

Blood

Quiz 18 · Healthy Living

QUESTIONS

ANSWERS

1 Which part of a tea plant is used to make tea?

The leaves

2 Can drinking alcohol make you ill?

Yes

3 Which form of cooking is healthiest – frying, steaming or roasting?

Steaming

4 Why is it unhealthy to eat too much cheese?

Because cheese contains a lot of fat

5 Which food is more likely to boost your brainpower – fish or chips?

Fish

It's a fact! Eating fish is good for you! Fish contains lots of protein and is low in fat and calories. Some fish contains special substances that may help to keep your heart healthy.

Picture Clue
Quiz 17
Question 9

6 If you cut your finger, what helps your blood to clot – platelets or dishlets?

Platelets

7 How many portions of fruit and vegetables should you aim to eat every day?

Five

8 Which is fastest – jogging, strolling, sprinting or trotting?

Sprinting

9 What would a doctor use to give you an injection?

A syringe

10 Where are your balance organs – in your ears or up your nose?

In your ears

Quiz 19 • Healthy Living

Food Groups

It's important to eat a well-balanced diet across a range of food groups. Look at these pictures and say which food group they belong to.

Carbohydrates • Dairy • Fats
Fruit and vegetables • Protein

ANSWERS Dairy: 3. Milk 9. Cheese Carbohydrates: 2. Rice 7. Bread Fruit and vegetables: 1. Grapes 6. Cauliflower Fats: 5. Butter 10. Nuts Protein: 4. Meat (beef) 8. Fish (salmon)

Name the Bones

Can you match the labels on the left to the skeleton?

Femur
Humerus
Patella
Pelvis
Radius
Rib cage
Skull
Spine
Sternum
Ulna

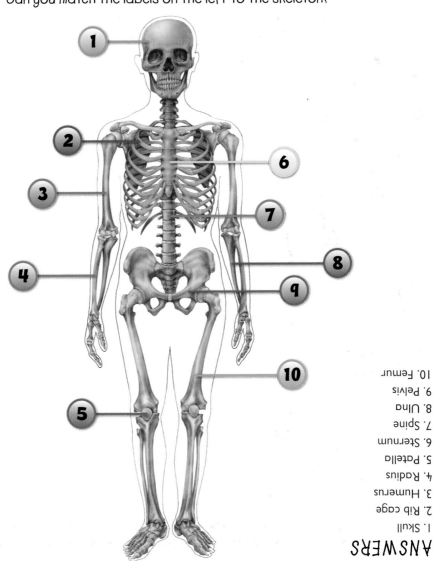

ANSWERS
1. Skull
2. Rib cage
3. Humerus
4. Radius
5. Patella
6. Sternum
7. Spine
8. Ulna
9. Pelvis
10. Femur

Quiz 21 • Wonderful Words

1 What is the fourth book in J K Rowling's series about Harry Potter?

Harry Potter and the Goblet of Fire

2 Spell 'necessary'.

Necessary

3 Is the sentence 'fat foxes can't fly fast' an example of alliteration or alteration?

Alliteration

4 What job title describes a person who plans how a book will look?

A designer

5 Does a biographer write about other people's lives, or about biology?

Other people's lives

It's a fact! A rainbow is an arc of colour that appears in the sky. It happens when rain is reflected by sunlight. Rainbow colours are red, orange, yellow, green, blue, indigo and violet.

Picture Clue
Quiz 22
Question 4

6 Crimson, scarlet, ruby and brick are all shades of what colour?

Red

7 What letter is silent in the word 'knife'?

K

8 Which electronic device can be used to download and read books – an e-book or e-words?

E-book

9 What is the collective noun for a group of sheep?

Flock

10 What is the American word for 'tap' – elevator or faucet?

Faucet

Quiz 22 • Wonderful Words

QUESTIONS

ANSWERS

1 Anna Sewell wrote the novel *Black Beauty* in 1877. What type of animal is Black Beauty?

A horse

2 What does the abbreviation ASAP stand for?

As soon as possible

3 What letter is silent in the word 'island'?

S

4 What type of creatures does Darren Shan write about in *Cirque du Freak* – vampires or zombies?

Vampires

5 Are the words 'he', 'she', 'you' and 'we' examples of proper nouns or pronouns?

Pronouns

It's a fact! *Black Beauty* tells the story of an ill-treated horse. Readers were so shocked and upset by the tale, they campaigned to improve conditions for working animals.

Picture Clue
QUIZ 21
Question 10

6 Which great British writer is sometimes called the Bard of Avon – William Shakespeare or Roald Dahl?

William Shakespeare

7 What is a verb?

An action word in a sentence

8 Synonyms are words that have the same, or similar meanings. Is 'honest' a synonym of 'truthful'?

Yes

9 Do adverbs tell us more about a verb or more about a noun?

A verb

10 What type of animal does the word 'canine' refer to?

Dog

Quiz 23 • Wonderful Words

QUESTIONS

ANSWERS

1 If something is described as 'shipshape' is it able to float or is it in a good and tidy condition?

In a good and tidy condition

2 Do proper nouns begin with capital letters?

Yes

3 How many letters are in the alphabet?

26

4 Who is the author of the bestselling *Inkheart* series of books – Cornflower Punk or Cornelia Funke?

Cornelia Funke

5 Spell 'successful'.

Successful

It's a fact! People used to decorate their homes with dead animals that had been stuffed by taxidermists. The word 'taxidermy' comes from the Greek words meaning 'arrangement of skin'.

Picture Clue
Quiz 24
Question 3

6 If the word 'maritime' refers to the sea, what type of bear has the Latin name *Ursus maritimus*?

Polar bear

7 What A is a collection of poems or songs – anthology or anthrax?

Anthology

8 A limerick is a humorous poem containing how many lines?

Five

9 Antonyms are words with opposite meanings. What word is an antonym of 'hot'?

Cold

10 What does a taxidermist do – tell people how much tax to pay or stuff dead animals?

Stuff dead animals

1 Who has illustrated most of Jacqueline Wilson's books – Anthony Browne or Nick Sharatt?

Nick Sharatt

2 Where would you find shingle – at a fishmonger's shop or on a beach?

On a beach

3 What is the first book in Michelle Paver's *Chronicles of Ancient Darkness* series – *Wolf Brother* or *Torak's Trek*?

Wolf Brother

4 Where would you find the index of a book?

At the back

5 Does 'amber' describe something that is a shade of orange or green?

Orange

It's a fact! There is a large vocabulary (collection of special words) that are connected with horses. The young are called foals, adult males are stallions and adult females are mares.

Picture Clue
Quiz 23 Question 6

6 Spell 'millennium'.

Millennium

7 What letter is silent in the word 'wrong'?

W

8 What word is the antonym of 'shut'?

Open

9 Spell 'vocabulary'.

Vocabulary

10 What is a filly – a purple-petalled flower or a young female horse?

A young female horse

Quiz 25 • Wonderful Words

1 In C S Lewis's *The Lion, the Witch and the Wardrobe*, what type of animal is Aslan?

A lion

2 Are Michael Rosen and Carol Ann Duffy poets or illustrators?

Poets

3 Which of these words does not have the letter U in it – guard, business, emperor or neighbour?

Emperor

4 In which Roald Dahl story does greedy Augustus Gloop fall into a lake of chocolate?

Charlie and the Chocolate Factory

5 Spell 'unfortunately'.

Unfortunately

It's a fact! Chocolate has been around for hundreds of years and is enjoyed by millions of people. However milk chocolate was not invented until 1876, in Switzerland.

Picture Clue
Quiz 26 Question 6

6 What letter is silent in the word 'calm'?

L

7 Where can you go to read, study and borrow books for free?

Library

8 How many 'S's are there in the word successes?

Four

9 List the five vowels in the alphabet.

A E I O U

10 Are words that begin with the prefix 'hydro-' usually to do with flying or with water?

Water

Quiz 26 • Wonderful Words

1 Do fiction books contain stories or facts?

Stories

2 In Anthony Horowitz's books about teenager Alex Rider, what does Alex Ryder do?

He's a spy

3 What name is given to a break in the middle of a play or performance?

Interval

4 What grisly thing do cannibals do?

Eat human flesh

5 Spell 'scissors'.

Scissors

It's a fact! The legend of Robin Hood has survived for hundreds of years. With his Merry Men, he stole from the rich to give to the poor – but no one knows if Robin ever really existed.

Picture Clue
Quiz 25
Question 1

6 Which young wizard's mail was addressed to 'The Cupboard under the Stairs, 4 Privet Drive'?

Harry Potter's

7 Are the tales of Robin Hood mythical or factual?

Mythical

8 What type of reference book contains lists of words that have similar meanings?

Thesaurus

9 How many consonants are in the alphabet?

21

10 Which of these words would come first in a dictionary – wholegrain, quick, honesty, knitting?

Honesty

Quiz 27 • Wonderful Words

1 In literature, which teenage crook takes on fairies, goblins and trolls – Artemis Fowl or Arcadia Grouse?

Artemis Fowl

2 Cyan, navy, indigo and royal are all shades of what colour?

Blue

3 Spell 'nightmare'.

Nightmare

4 If something is described as 'feline' is it like a cat or a dog?

Cat

5 Does a semi-colon have two dots, or one dot and a comma?

One dot and a comma

It's a fact! Lewis Carroll (1832–1898) is most famous for his stories Alice in Wonderland and Through the Looking Glass, but he also wrote the famous nonsense poem, Jabberwocky.

Picture Clue
Quiz 28
Question 3

6 If an author has written a trilogy, how many books have they written?

Three

7 Who wrote about the Jabberwocky – Lewis Hamilton or Lewis Carroll?

Lewis Carroll

8 What is the platform called where actors perform in a theatre?

Stage

9 Mambo, tango, salsa and jive are all types of what?

Dance

10 What term is used for the person who creates the artwork that is used in a picture book?

Illustrator or artist

Quiz 28 • Wonderful Words

1 Spell 'Wednesday'.

Wednesday

2 What letter is silent in the word 'castle'?

T

3 What type of party does Alice attend in Wonderland?

A tea party

4 Who wrote about the tragic events that befell the Baudelaire children in *A Series of Unfortunate Events*?

Lemony Snicket

5 What type of reference book contains alphabetical lists of words and their meanings?

Dictionary

It's a fact! Fathoms are used to measure depth underwater. One fathom is 1.8 metres, and the word comes from an old English word meaning the length of outstretched arms.

Picture Clue
Quiz 27
Question 4

6 Where would you be if depth was being measured in fathoms – at sea or up a mountain?

At sea

7 Synonyms are words that have the same, or similar meanings. Is 'stumble' a synonym of 'falter'?

Yes

8 In a theatre, what name is given to the large group of people who watch a play?

Audience

9 Spell 'restaurant'.

Restaurant

10 What name is given to the conversation, or the lines, spoken by characters in a story or play?

Dialogue

Identify the Idiom

An idiom is a phrase that has a different meaning to the one that the words suggest.

Look at these idioms. What do they mean?

1 As good as gold

2 Over the moon

3 Pull someone's leg

4 Put your foot in it

5 Move heaven and earth

6 As old as the hills

7 To pay through the nose

8 Crocodile tears

9 Too big for your boots

10 Knock me down with a feather

Collective Nouns

Each of these animal groups has its own name, or collective noun. Choose the correct word to describe each set of animals.

1. Pod or herd
2. Shoal or colony
3. Pack or mob
4. Brood or clowder
5. Troop or gaggle
6. Shoal or colony
7. Brood or clowder
8. Pack or mob
9. Pod or herd
10. Troop or gaggle

ANSWERS 1. Herd of hippos 2. Shoal of fish 3. Mob of kangaroos 4. Clowder of kittens 5. Troop of monkeys 6. Colony of ants 7. Brood of chicks 8. Pack of wolves 9. Pod of dolphins 10. Gaggle of geese

Quiz 31 • Super Science

1 When a liquid evaporates, does it disappear or turn into a gas?

It turns into a gas

2 What makes sound when you whistle – rhythm or vibration?

Vibration

3 What type of rock allows water to pass through it – practical rock or permeable rock?

Permeable

4 Which force is caused by gravity pulling down on a mass?

Weight

5 Where can a poisonous liquid metal be found – in a thermometer or thermostat?

Thermometer

It's a fact! A skydiver leaping from a plane at 4000 metres won't open his parachute until about 1500 metres from the ground. Then he'll slow down so quickly, he'll feel like he's shooting upwards.

Picture Clue
Quiz 32
Question 7

6 Why aren't oven gloves made from tin foil?

Metal conducts heat, so you'd get burnt

7 Which is easiest to squash – a gas or a liquid?

A gas

8 What are cirrus, stratus and cumulus types of?

Clouds

9 Which of these is not part of a simple electrical circuit – a battery, a bulb, a brake or a buzzer?

A brake

10 When a skydiver's parachute opens, what increases – gravity or air resistance?

Air resistance

Quiz 32 • Super Science

1 What is an empty space with no particles of solid, liquid or gas – a vacuum or a hoover?

A vacuum

2 Will oiling a spring make it work better?

No

3 What would you use to separate dissolved sugar from water – evaporation or condensation?

Evaporation

4 Does something keep moving until the force runs out, or until another force stops it?

Until another force stops it

5 Can you make an electrical plug entirely out of plastic?

No, only metal pins conduct electricity

It's a fact! Our bodies regulate temperature, so we remain at 37°C. In the Arctic, explorers' bodies can't always cope. They can die if their body temperature drops by just 2°C.

Picture Clue
Quiz 31
Question 5

6 Are particles of matter further apart in a solid, a liquid or a gas?

A gas

7 I am a slippery, squashy substance used to make candles. What am I?

Wax

8 What is the temperature inside our bodies – 73°C or 37°C?

37°C

9 Does chalk float?

No

10 What stops gravity pulling us into the ground – another force pushing up from the ground or magnetism?

Another force pushing up from the ground

Quiz 33 • Super Science

QUESTIONS

ANSWERS

1 Is orange squash transparent, opaque or translucent?

Translucent

2 Which hard rock did Stone Age people use for axe blades?

Flint

3 Is the River Thames part of the world's water cycle?

Yes

4 What name is given to a material that allows heat to pass through it easily?

Thermal conductor

5 Is there gravity on the Sun?

Yes

It's a fact! The sound of thunder travels at 300 metres per second, so it takes a few seconds to reach us. Light is about one million times faster, so we see lightning almost at once.

Picture Clue
Quiz 34
Question 4

6 Is something that dissolves in water soluble or syllable?

Soluble

7 Does a dog reflect light?

Yes, otherwise it would be invisible!

8 Do all musical instruments vibrate?

Yes

9 Thunder is the noise of lightning. Do we see or hear it first?

We see it first

10 Why can't electricity flow across a gap in a circuit – because air is a bad electrical conductor or a bad electrical insulator?

A bad electrical conductor

Quiz 34 • Super Science

QUESTIONS

ANSWERS

1 Does oil dissolve in water?

No, it floats

2 When the Sun's shadows are shortest, is the Sun overhead or on the horizon?

Overhead

3 When a gas is cooled, what does it change into first — a liquid or a solid?

A liquid

4 I am an impermeable rock the ancient Greeks and Romans used to make statues. What am I?

Marble

5 What kind of rain can damage buildings and trees?

Acid rain

It's a fact! The Taj Mahal in India is one of the Seven Wonders of the World. It took 20,000 people 21 years to build, and the marble was transported by teams of Asian elephants.

Picture Clue
Quiz 33
Question 2

6 Why doesn't a fish sink — because it is absorbent, buoyant or optimistic?

Buoyant

7 Is it possible to use wind to generate electricity?

Yes

8 Why are electrical wires coated in plastic?

To make them safer

9 Is the shape of a Formula One racing car aerobic or aerodynamic?

Aerodynamic

10 Which would make the darker shadow — a piece of tissue paper or a piece of newspaper?

A piece of newspaper

Quiz 35 • Super Science

1 What is happening to a liquid that is cooling and turning into a solid?

It is starting to freeze

2 What planet is known as the Red Planet?

Mars

3 Which scientist was named as 'man of the century' in 1999 – Isaac Newton or Albert Einstein?

Albert Einstein – Isaac Newton died in 1727

4 Would you slide further down a gentle slope or a steep slope?

A steep slope

5 What is the name of the rubbing force between two objects?

Friction

It's a fact! A catamaran is a boat with two hulls, or main bodies. The hulls are connected by one or two decks. Catamarans often take part in races.

Picture Clue
Quiz 36
Question 3

6 Where would you find your vertebrae – on your ribs or on your spine?

On your spine, they're are bones

7 Which has the darker shadow – something that's opaque or something that's translucent?

Something that's opaque

8 Which material is better at absorbing sound – carpet or polished wood?

Carpet

9 Where would you find a catamaran – on the road, in the air or on water?

On water – it's a type of boat

10 A hot cup of tea is left overnight in a room where the air temperature is 20°C. What is the tea's temperature the next morning?

20°C

Quiz 36 • Super Science

QUESTIONS

ANSWERS

1 What force makes a compass work – gravity or magnetism?

Magnetism

2 Does a potato conduct electricity?

Yes, because it has lots of water in it

3 I come from trees. I am a squashy, bendy, material and a good electrical insulator. What am I?

Rubber

4 What name is given to the dark, crumbly soil made up of plants that died thousands of ago?

Peat

5 What might you measure with a forcemeter – the strength of a pull or the loudness of a sound?

The strength of a pull

It's a fact! Liquid oxygen is used to propel rockets into space. It can be kept at temperatures above –183°C, but only by squashing it very hard. Otherwise it boils and turns back into a gas.

Picture Clue
Quiz 35
Question 3

6 Which would reflect light best – a brown bear, a polar bear or a panda?

A polar bear – because it is white

7 Does oxygen turn from a gas to a liquid at 183°C or –183°C?

–183°C

8 Why do you weigh more on Earth than on the Moon – because there is less wind or more gravity?

More gravity

9 Is our skin waterproof?

Yes

10 What is the opposite of condensation – freezing or evaporation?

Evaporation

Quiz 37 • Super Science

1 What condenses to form a liquid – a gas or a solid?

A gas

2 Can you make wool from goat fur?

Yes, cashmere and mohair wools

3 What does gradient measure?

How steep a slope is

4 Which is an irreversible change – dissolving salt in water or grilling a steak?

Grilling a steak

5 What opens and closes a gap in an electrical circuit?

A switch

It's a fact! Cashmere wool is very soft and warm, but it's also expensive. Cashmere goats also have rough hair, which is only separated from the soft fibres by hours and hours of combing.

Picture Clue
Quiz 38
Question 9

6 Can you measure someone's weight when they're standing on the floor?

No

7 What are the primary colours of light?

Red, green and blue

8 If a plane travels west, in which direction does air resistance act on it?

East

9 Is plastic a good conductor of electricity?

No

10 To remove salt from sand, would you filter it first, or add water?

Add water first (to dissolve it)

1 Does hot air rise or fall?

Rise

2 Why can you slide further on a polished wooden floor than on a carpeted floor?

Because there's less friction

3 Which force keeps the Moon orbiting the Earth and the Earth orbiting the Moon?

Gravity

4 Is iron extracted from rock or is it made from dead plants and animals?

Extracted from rock

5 Is a wooden door opaque or translucent?

Opaque

It's a fact! Along with the Moon, thousands of man-made satellites orbit Earth. Some do useful things, like take pictures and send TV signals, but many are bits of rubbish, known as space junk.

Picture Clue

Quiz 37 Question 3

20%

6 When you throw a ball up in the air, what force pulls it down?

Gravity

7 Which of these instruments usually has a spring – a forcemeter or a thermometer?

A forcemeter

8 Is cork a good insulator of electricity or sound?

Both

9 Which soft white rock is made from the skeletons of tiny sea animals?

Chalk

10 Which natural material is strongest – silk or string?

Silk

In the Laboratory

A scientist uses lots of different equipment in a laboratory. Match the names of these pieces of equipment with the pictures.

Bunsen burner, condenser, flask, goggles, microscope, pestle and mortar, petri dish, pipette, test tubes, tongs.

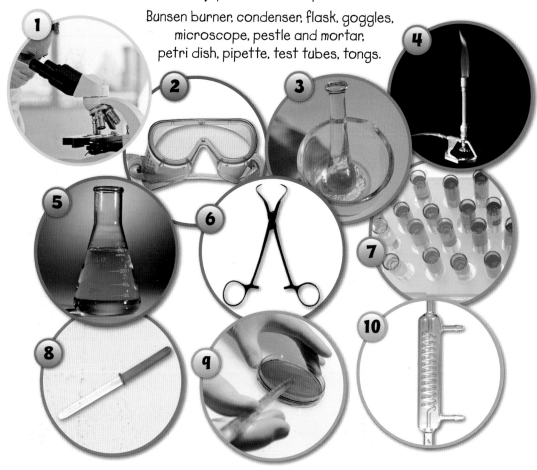

Match the Scientist

Different types of scientist study different things.
Look at the pictures and labels. Can you match
the scientist to the area of study?

Archaeologist, astronomer, botanist, cartographer,
geologist, mathematician, meteorologist,
palaeontologist, volcanologist, zoologist.

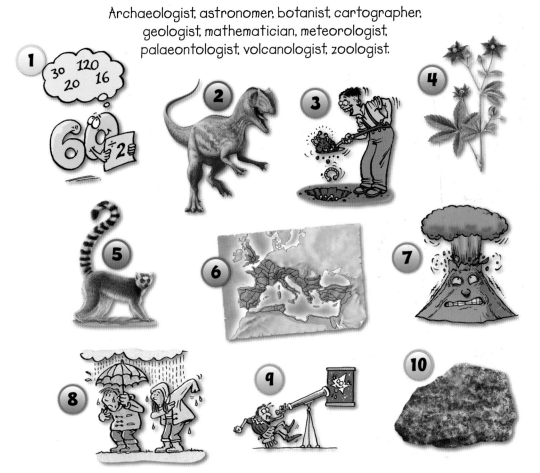

Quiz 41 • Number Crunchers

1 What is a grid's horizontal axis called – the x-axis or the a-axis?

x-axis

2 Are feet and inches known as imperial or imperative measurements?

Imperial

3 What is the square of 6?

36

4 What does a small letter 'd' become if you look at it in a mirror?

A small letter 'b'

5 How many equal sides does an equilateral triangle have?

Three

It's a fact! Most of the world uses the metric system to measure distance, mass and capacity. But a few countries, including the UK and US still use miles for road distances and speeds.

50 km/h

Picture Clue
Quiz 42
Question 10

6 What is 25% as a fraction?

¼ (one-quarter)

7 A film starts at 18.45 and goes on for 1½ hours. What time does it finish?

20.15

8 Adam's hand luggage weighs 6820 grams. Is this more than the airline's 12 kilograms limit?

No, 6820 grams is only 6.8 kilograms

9 What C is another word for probability?

Chance

10 Round up 758 to the nearest hundred.

800

1 Which cross at right angles – parallel lines or perpendicular lines?

Perpendicular lines

2 Is 3 a factor of 21, or is 21 a factor of 3?

3 is a factor of 21

3 Divide 56 by 8.

7

4 A diver does a somersault and then enters the water headfirst. How many degrees has he turned?

540°

5 What is 0.4 x 3?

1.2

It's a fact! Being large at the bottom and small at the top, pyramids are very stable. So early civilizations were able to build huge structures without using complicated engineering designs.

Picture Clue
Quiz 41
Question 5

6 Does a square-based pyramid have an equal number of sides and vertices?

Yes, it has five of each

7 What is one-hundredth of a metre called?

A centimetre

8 Patrick scored 60% in his geography test. If there were 10 questions, how many did he get right?

Six

9 What type of chart is round – a pie chart or a ball chart?

A pie chart

10 What do you use to measure an angle – a compass or a protractor?

A protractor

Quiz 43 • number Crunchers

1 Which letter can you rotate by 180° without changing it – V, S or C?

S

2 On a graph, is the y-axis horizontal or vertical?

Vertical

3 What is larger – 60%, or 25 out of 50?

60% – 25 out of 50 is half, or 50%

4 What's the chance of rolling a 6 on a dice?

One in six

5 What is a 2D shape with five sides called?

A pentagon

It's a fact! The world famous Pentagon near Washington D.C. is the home of the United States Department of Defense. About 23,000 people work there, although they're not all soldiers.

Picture Clue
Quiz 44
Question 4

6 What is 785 divided by 4 – about 300 or about 200?

About 200

7 What is a half of one-third?

One-sixth

8 What is the next number in this sequence: 48, 40, 32 … ?

24 (there is 8 less each time)

9 What is a parallelogram with all four sides equal called – a kite or a rhombus?

A rhombus

10 What is 50% of 180?

90

Quiz 44 • number Crunchers

1 If two of a triangle's angles are 60°, how big is the third angle?

60° – a triangle's angles add up to 180°

2 Divide 49 by 7.

7

3 If the square of 4 is 16, what is the square of 5?

25

4 How tall is a giraffe – about 6 metres or 12 metres?

About 6 metres

5 Is a fence that goes all the way around a field called a perimeter or a radius fence?

A perimeter fence

It's a fact! The perimeter of a circle is called its circumference. The distance around the Earth's Equator is about 40,000 kilometres – this is the circumference of the Earth.

Picture Clue
Quiz 43
Question 9

6 Which is not a metric unit – gram, stone, litre or millimetre?

Stone

7 What's the missing number in this sequence – 63, 54, ..., 36, 27?

45 (there is 9 less each time)

8 What is an angle between 90° and 180° called – obtuse or obese?

Obtuse

9 If you move an object to different coordinates, is it called transforming or teleporting?

Transforming

10 How many litres of water might an average bath hold – 9 litres or 90 litres?

90 litres

Quiz 45 • Number Crunchers

1 What's the probability of the Sun rising tomorrow, as a percentage?

100%

2 What is the capacity of a litre-measuring jug?

One litre

3 Scott has a pizza. He gives himself half then gives the rest to two friends. How much do they get each?

One-quarter

4 How many days are in four weeks?

28

5 Which is not a way of presenting data – a graph, a chair or a table?

A chair

It's a fact! Quad bikes are like motorbikes, but they have four wheels instead of two. They are useful for driving on rough ground, so some farmers use them to get about on their land.

Picture Clue
Quiz 46
Question 3

6 Kate did a headstand for 3 minutes and 20 seconds. How many seconds was that altogether?

200

7 What is the only factor of the number 49?

7

8 What are the four areas on a grid called – quadrupeds or quadrants?

Quadrants

9 What is 250 divided by 5?

50

10 If one mouse weighs 10 grams, how many mice would weigh one-tenth of a kilogram?

10

Quiz 46 • number Crunchers

1 How many parallel lines are there in the letter M?

Two

2 What is a corner of a 3D shape called?

A vertex

3 Which of these is an old calculating tool – an abacus or a bacillus?

An abacus

4 How many centimetres in one metre?

100

5 Which of these units can't be used to measure milk – kilograms, gallons, centimetres or litres?

Centimetres

It's a fact! Although Egyptian mathematicians invented the abacus in about 2000 BC, pocket calculators weren't invented until the 1970s. People used to do much more maths in their heads!

Picture Clue
Quiz 45
Question 3

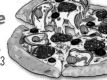

6 What is ¾ as a decimal?

0.75

7 How many legs do 11 giraffes have?

44

8 Does a reflex angle measure exactly 180°, or more than 180°?

More than 180°

9 Which is longer, 100 metres or one mile?

One mile – it is 1609 metres

10 Double 75 and subtract 40. What is your answer?

110

Quiz 47 • number Crunchers

1 Mary was born in 1937. In what year did she celebrate her 70th birthday?

2007

2 How many degrees do you need to rotate the letter Z to get an N?

90°

3 What's the next number in this sequence: 0.75, 0.65, 0.55 …?

0.45 (each number decreases by 0.1)

4 What is 368,357 as a round number?

368,000

5 What's the distance from the outside to the centre of a circle – the radius or the diameter?

The radius

It's a fact! In many parts of the world, 1st April is known as April Fools' Day. It is a day when people may play practical jokes on friends and family.

Picture Clue
Quiz 48
Question 2

6 Divide 54 by 9.

6

7 What do the angles in a quadrilateral always add up to – 180° or 360°?

360°

8 Which type of triangle has two equal sides and two equal angles?

Isosceles

9 It is 25th March. What is the date in exactly one week's time

1st April

10 Ben divides a packet of peanuts between himself and two friends. There are 42 peanuts. How many do they each get?

14

Quiz 48 • Number Crunchers

1 What type of triangle has two perpendicular lines?

A right-angled triangle

2 If you're pointing North and turn 90° anti-clockwise, which way are you pointing?

West

3 What is the mass of an average cat – 50 kilograms or 5 kilograms?

5 kilograms

4 How many hundreds are there in the number 4210?

42

5 What is one-third of 33?

11

It's a fact! At 21.2 kilograms, Himmy held a world record as the heaviest cat. But the Guinness Book of Records has now removed the category to discourage people from overfeeding their cats.

Picture Clue
Quiz 47
Question 8

6 Which statement is true: 'a rhombus is a parallelogram' or 'a parallelogram is a rhombus'?

A rhombus is a parallelogram

7 A square measures 2 centimetres by 3 centimetres. What is its area?

6 centimetres squared

8 What is longer – a mile or a kilometre?

A mile

9 What are the units on a protractor – millimetres or degrees?

Degrees

10 I buy a kite for £15.98 with a £20 note. How much change do I get?

£4.02

Pictures in a Spin

Each of these photographs has been rotated. Some have been rotated by 45°, some by 90° and some by 180°.

Can you work out how much each one has been rotated?

Get Measuring!

There are lots of different devices for measuring things. First, name the instruments below. Then work out what they measure using this list:

Air pressure, angles, length, speed, temperature, time, volume, weight.

1 **2** **3** **4** **5** **6** **7** **8** **9** **10**

Quiz 51 • Our World

1 Kalahari, Gobi and Mojave are all types of what – desert or lake?

Desert

2 On a ship, does port mean 'left-hand side' or 'right-hand side'?

Left-hand side

3 Is the North Pole covered by land or by frozen ocean?

Frozen ocean

4 Which rubber parts of a car might be recycled to make a soft surface for a playground?

Tyres

5 What name is given to a spinning column of wind that moves at great speed?

Tornado

It's a fact! Tornadoes form when air in a thundercloud begins to spin. A swirling funnel of air reaches to the ground, sucking up objects and destroying houses and cars in its path.

Picture Clue
Quiz 52
Question 1

6 If you travelled south from Britain, which continent would you reach first – Antarctica or Africa?

Africa

7 Does the Sun rise in the east or in the west?

In the east

8 If a population increases does it mean there are more people or towns in an area?

More people

9 Which nation produces the most films every year – India or the USA?

India

10 Who is the chairman of the computer software company Microsoft – and is one of the richest men in the world?

Bill Gates

Quiz 52 • Our World

1 What is the world's most used fuel – oil or coal?

Oil

2 What mineral is found in large amounts in seawater, but not in freshwater?

Salt

3 When is noon – midday or midnight?

Midday

4 If someone works in agriculture do they work on a farm or in a hospital?

On a farm

5 What name is given to a region in Great Britain, such as Devon, Cumbria or Suffolk?

County

It's a fact! About 70 million barrels of oil are pumped out of the Earth every day, to supply around 35 percent of the world's energy. Saudi Arabia has the biggest oil reserves.

Picture Clue
Quiz 51
Question 4

6 Which continent covers one-third of the world's land – Asia or Europe?

Asia

7 What is made from rotting green waste, such as plant cuttings and vegetable peelings?

Compost

8 What is a severe snowstorm – a buzzard or a blizzard?

Blizzard

9 Are there any mountains at the North Pole?

No

10 Which of these is a greenhouse gas, which adds to the problem of global warming: oxygen, carbon dioxide or helium?

Carbon dioxide

Quiz 53 • Our World

1 2012 will be a leap year. When will the next leap year occur after then?

2016

2 What method of transport looks like a train but runs on rails that are dug into roads?

Tram

3 Where did potatoes first grow — South America or Africa?

South America

4 What is a rickshaw?

A form of transport powered by people

5 Which of these countries does not border India — Pakistan, Bangladesh or Botswana?

Botswana

It's a fact! Rickshaws are vehicles that are powered by people, not by engines or animals. They can be pulled by people running, or on bicycles. Modern rickshaws are sometimes called pedicabs.

Picture Clue
Quiz 54
Question 2

6 What is the centre of the Earth called — the core or the crust?

The core

7 Which flying vehicle has rotor blades rather than wings?

A helicopter

8 Is New York on the east coast of the USA, or the west coast?

East coast

9 Is a glacier a river of ice or giant floating iceberg?

A river of ice

10 What is the world's largest ocean?

Pacific

Quiz 54 • Our World

1 Is *Sahara* the Arabic word for 'desert' or 'jungle'?

Desert

2 What is the largest planet in the Solar System?

Jupiter

3 Which are deeper – seas or oceans?

Oceans

4 What name is given to the groups of stars that make patterns in the night sky?

Constellations

5 How many Americans speak Spanish as their first language – 28,000 or 28 million?

28 million

It's a fact! There are 88 constellations, or groups of stars, in the night sky, such as The Great Bear and Orion, the Hunter. In the past, sailors used constellations to guide them on their journeys.

Picture Clue
Quiz 53
Question 7

6 What force do Maglev trains use to power them – gravity or magnetism?

Magnetism

7 In which country might you be called a Pom while enjoying some tucker at a barbie?

Australia

8 What machine moves people up and down between the floors of a building?

A lift

9 Saloons, hatchbacks, estates and four-by-fours are all types of what?

Car

10 What rocky body orbits the Earth every 29.5 days?

The Moon

Quiz 55 • Our World

1 What is the world's largest rainforest?

The Amazon

2 Does pollution increase or decrease the amount of greenhouse gases in our atmosphere?

Increase

3 Do we use the term a.m. for times in the evening or in the morning?

Morning

4 What is the capital city of Belgium?

Brussels

5 In which country might you visit the Taj Mahal?

India

It's a fact! Biofuels are made out of plant materials. Not many countries have their own fossil fuels, such as oil and coal, so growing and making biofuels can be cheaper and more reliable.

Picture Clue
Quiz 56
Question 3

6 What type of fuel is made from plants such as rape and sugar beet – biofuel or geofuel?

Biofuel

7 If you travelled east through Europe, which continent would you reach first – Asia or South America?

Asia

8 How long does it take the Earth to orbit the Sun?

365 days

9 Which large African reptile is associated with the river Nile?

The Nile crocodile

10 How many months are in one-quarter of a year?

Three

Quiz 56 • Our World

1 What two countries are linked by the Channel Tunnel?

France and England

2 If someone works in manufacturing do they work on a ship or in a factory?

In a factory

3 What is the world's tallest mountain on land?

Mount Everest

4 How many countries are in the world – 193 or 93?

193

5 How long does it take the Earth to spin once around its own axis?

24 hours

It's a fact! A passenger plane cruises at a height of 37,000 feet – that's just over 11 kilometres! Aircraft are designed to be as streamlined as possible to reduce drag and save on fuel.

Picture Clue
Quiz 55
Question 9

6 Which European country is the best in the world at recycling rubbish – Switzerland or Wales?

Switzerland

7 Where do most passenger planes fly to meet least air resistance – below the clouds or above them?

Above

8 Which ocean is closest to the Antarctic – the Southern Ocean or the Arctic Ocean?

The Southern Ocean

9 What type of boat carries oil around the world – tankers or yachts?

Tankers

10 How many days are in a leap year?

366

Quiz 57 • Our World

1 Which metal is extracted from rocks and used to make drinks cans – aluminium or mercury?

Aluminium

2 Which of these animals would you not see in an African wildlife reserve – lions, pandas or zebras?

Pandas

3 What name is given to a moving staircase?

Escalator

4 Which continent is the birthplace of many religions, including Christianity, Buddhism, Islam and Judaism?

Asia

5 What is the seventh month of the year?

July

It's a fact! Drinks cans are made from aluminium – a strong, light metal. Recycling is easy and quite cheap, and uses just 5 percent of the energy needed to make cans from new aluminium.

Picture Clue
Quiz 58
Question 10

6 If you dig deep into the Earth does the temperature around you get hotter or colder?

Hotter

7 Are the Rockies a chain of mountains or a series of giant waterfalls?

A chain of mountains

8 What is the most common gas in our atmosphere?

Nitrogen

9 Do subway trains run above cities or below them?

Below

10 What is the world's longest mountain chain called – the Andes or the Alps?

The Andes

Quiz 58 • Our World

1 What tiny eco-friendly cars have become popular in crowded cities – Smart cars or Bright cars?

Smart cars

2 What occurs when the Earth's plates move against one another?

An earthquake

3 What would you use to measure the amount of rain – a barometer or a rain gauge?

A rain gauge

4 Does Mexico have a border with the USA or Russia?

The USA

5 The longest river in the USA is the Mississippi. How many letter 's's are in 'Mississippi'?

Four

It's a fact! Even hot deserts are very cold at night because there are no clouds in the sky. Clouds help to trap the heat close to the ground – without them all the heat escapes into space.

Picture Clue
Quiz 57
Question 2

6 What is the largest country in South America – Ecuador or Brazil?

Brazil

7 If you were standing on top of Mount Everest, which mountain range would you be looking at?

The Himalayas

8 If you spent the night in a desert would you feel hot or cold?

Cold

9 Which country has the most universities – India or Japan?

India

10 What is the world's most common farm animal?

Chicken

Quiz 59 • Our World

Water Power

Different types of watercraft
are powered in different ways.

Can you tell whether the watercraft
shown here are powered by wind,
a person or an engine?

Quiz 60 • Our World

Around the UK

The UK has many world-famous attractions. In which country would you find each of these landmarks – England, Wales, Northern Ireland or Scotland?

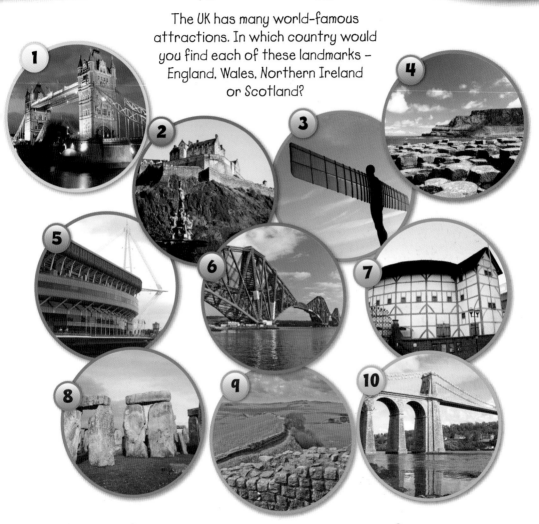

Quiz 61 • Past Times

1 Which English Queen was sometimes called Good Queen Bess?

Queen Elizabeth I

2 Was Woden a god of the Anglo-Saxons or the ancient Egyptians?

Anglo-Saxons

3 Did the year 560 BC happen before or after AD 335?

Before

4 Who was Henry VIII's father?

Henry VII

5 What underwater crafts were also known as U-boats in World War II?

Submarines

It's a fact! The Mini was designed to use less petrol than other cars and it eventually became the best-selling British car in history. In 40 years, more than five million Minis were sold.

Picture Clue

Quiz 62
Question 1

6 Which Christopher travelled to America in 1492 – Columbus or Colorado?

Columbus

7 Which small British car was designed by Alec Issigonis in 1957?

Mini

8 What century are we in – the 20th or the 21st?

21st

9 Which ancient people from North Africa mummified dead people and animals?

Egyptians

10 Was the penny farthing a type of bicycle or a bag of sweets?

A type of bicycle

Quiz 62 • Past Times

1 What were the kings of ancient Egypt called?

Pharaohs

2 Hitler's air attacks on Britain were called the Blitzkrieg. What is this time better known as?

The Blitz

3 What type of book did Anne Frank write?

A diary

4 In 1815, the Duke of Wellington defeated which French leader at the Battle of Waterloo?

Napoleon Bonaparte

5 In Tudor times, what was Hans Holbein famous for?

Painting

It's a fact! Anne Frank was a Jewish girl who hid from the Nazis during World War II. She was captured and died in a concentration camp, but her diary is one of the world's most read books.

Picture Clue
QUIZ 61
Question 1

6 What collection of jewels is kept in the Tower of London?

The Crown Jewels

7 In 1897, Queen Victoria celebrated her Diamond Jubilee. How many years had she been on the throne?

60

8 In 1951, which large exhibition opened in London to encourage the building of new towns?

Festival of Britain

9 When did people first use pocket calculators – the 1970s or the 1990s?

The 1970s

10 How many years are in one millennium?

1000

Quiz 63 • Past Times

1 In the Second World War, what name was given to the countries who fought together against Hitler?

The Allies

2 Since the 1920s, what famous industry in the US is based in Hollywood?

The film industry

3 When did early Britons begin to build Stonehenge – 500 or 5000 years ago?

5000 years ago

4 Where did Neil Armstrong take 'one small step for man' in 1969?

On the Moon

5 During the Second World War, were children evacuated to the countryside or to cities?

The countryside

It's a fact! The first Stonehenge was simply a round ditch with two large stones. Over 2000 years it became an enormous stone circle that may have been used as a place of worship.

Picture Clue
Quiz 64
Question 7

6 Which famous Scottish king defeated the English at the Battle of Bannockburn in 1314?

Robert the Bruce

7 How long did the Hundred Years War last?

116 years!

8 When the Romans invaded Britain, what did they call their new territory?

Britannia

9 Who was the British leader during the Second World War?

Winston Churchill

10 Daimler, Benz and Ford are famous makers of what type of vehicle?

Cars

Quiz 64 • Past Times

1 In the Second World War, what name is given to 6th June 1944 (Allies landed on Normandy beaches)?

D-Day

2 Which English king was also known as 'Lionheart' – Henry VIII or Richard I?

Richard I

3 What M describes heads of state such as kings, queens and emperors?

Monarchs

4 Who invented paper – the Chinese or the Vikings?

The Chinese

5 Which of these foods was not rationed in the Second World War – eggs, potatoes, butter or sugar?

Potatoes

It's a fact! On D-Day, Allied troops landed in Normandy, France. Many died in battles on the beaches. Eventually Europe was freed and the Second World War was over.

Picture Clue
Quiz 63
Question 4

6 Which ancient people had religious leaders called druids – Celts or Romans?

Celts

7 On which continent did the first humans evolve?

Africa

8 Did the Battle of the Somme take place in the First or Second World War?

First World War

9 What game was invented in India about 2000 years ago and has pieces called knights, pawns and bishops?

Chess

10 Which metal was used first to make weapons – bronze or iron?

Iron

Quiz 65 • Past Times

QUESTIONS

ANSWERS

1 Are the Romans famous for building straight roads or roundabouts?

Straight roads

2 In what year did the Second World War break out – 1914 or 1939?

1939

3 In which ancient country did the Olympic Games begin?

Ancient Greece

4 What name is given to the time when people made tools and weapons from stone?

The Stone Age

5 What country is famous for its samurai warriors?

Japan

It's a fact! King Offa could not defeat the Celts in Wales so he dug a ditch and built a bank of earth, 270 kilometres long, to keep them out of England.

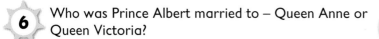

Picture Clue

QUIZ 66
Question 8

6 Who was Prince Albert married to – Queen Anne or Queen Victoria?

Queen Victoria

7 With which Egyptian queen did the Roman general Julius Caesar fall in love with?

Cleopatra

8 How many children did Elizabeth I have?

None

9 Which Saxon ruler became known as 'King of all England' – King Offa or King Henry?

King Offa

10 In 1918, which disease spread around the world killing millions of people – German measles or Spanish flu?

Spanish flu

Quiz 66 • Past Times

1 Who was the US leader during the Second World War – George W Bush or Franklin D Roosevelt?

Franklin D Roosevelt

2 What was a quill pen made from – fur or a feather?

A feather

3 What P was a terrible disease that was spread to humans by the fleas living on rats?

Plague

4 A statue of Admiral Lord Nelson is found in London's Trafalgar Square. Which sea battle did Nelson win?

The Battle of Trafalgar in 1805

5 What A is the country where British convicts were sent about 200 years ago?

Australia

It's a fact! The USA joined the Second World War after Japan attacked Pearl Harbor. Japan surrendered in 1945, after the US dropped devastating atom bombs on two cities.

Picture Clue
Quiz 65
Question 6

6 Who tried to blow up King James and parliament in 1605 – Guy Fawkes or Gus Knives?

Guy Fawkes

7 Who wrote the first history of England and is known as 'the Father of English history' – Bobble or Bede?

Bede

8 Which William is a famous Tudor playwright who wrote Romeo and Juliet?

Shakespeare

9 What type of footwear is named after the Duke of Wellington?

Wellington boots

10 Which material was used for building castles – rock or concrete?

Rock

Quiz 67 • Past Times

1 Who did Anne Boleyn and Anne of Cleves both marry?

Henry VIII

2 What type of boats were used by the Vikings?

Longboats

3 Which of these was not a British prime minister – Winston Churchill, John F Kennedy or Tony Blair

John F Kennedy

4 In 219 BC, who travelled across the Alps with his army and 40 war elephants?

Hannibal

5 How was Mary Queen of Scots related to Elizabeth I – was she her cousin or her aunt?

She was her cousin

It's a fact! The NHS was set up in 1948 to provide free healthcare to everyone. Before then, people had to pay for their treatments – this is still the system in most other countries.

Picture Clue
Quiz 68
Question 3

6 In 1845, what important crop failed, causing 1.5 million people in Ireland to die of starvation?

Potatoes

7 Which Victorian nurse was known as The Lady of the Lamp?

Florence Nightingale

8 In 1912, what caused the sinking of the ship *Titanic*?

It hit an iceberg

9 The NHS began in 1948. What do the letters NHS stand for?

National Health Service

10 What did Dick Turpin do for a living?

He was a highwayman

Quiz 68 • Past Times

1 In what year did did the Battle of Hastings take place?

1066

2 How many houses were destroyed in Britain during the Second World War – 5000 or 500,000?

500,000

3 What did Howard Carter discover in 1922 in Egypt?

Tutankhamun's tomb

4 Is a Spitfire a type of plane or tank?

Plane

5 Which king reigned after George I and before George III?

George II

It's a fact! Spitfires were fighter planes that were used during the Second World War. They were fast, reliable and agile. Spitfires still appear in classic aircraft displays.

Picture Clue
Quiz 67
Question 7

6 Which British city was built by the Romans along the River Thames and was called Londonium?

London

7 When did the British parliament vote to stop the buying and selling of human beings – 1807 or 1907?

1807

8 What enormous fleet of Spanish ships was sent to invade England in 1588 – Armageddon or Armada?

Armada

9 Around which river did the ancient Egyptians build their civilization?

River Nile

10 Who witnessed the Great Fire of London in 1666 – Queen Victoria or Samuel Pepys?

Samuel Pepys

Quiz 69 • Past Times

Famous People of the Past

Look at these famous historical people.

Can you guess who they are
from the clues below?

1

A British warrior-queen

2

A British scientist

3

A native American
war chief

4

A Scottish outlaw

5

A British admiral

6

A medieval English king

7

An Egyptian Queen

8

A Portuguese explorer

9

A French peasant girl

10

A Scottish prince

Quiz 70 • Past Times

Wonders of Rome

Can you match the pictures of these famous landmarks in Rome to their names?

Circus Maximus, Colosseum, The Pantheon, Roman Forum, Sistine Chapel, Spanish Steps, St Peter's Basilica, Trajan's Column, Trevi Fountain, Vatican City

Quiz 71 • How We Live

QUESTIONS

ANSWERS

1 What type of hat might a cowboy wear – a Pretzel or a Stetson?

A Stetson

2 Which Greek hero had to perform 12 terrible tasks, including killing the Hydra?

Hercules

3 What does a census count – the population of a country or the number of cars in a household?

The population of a country

4 What sport are Venus and Serena Williams famous for playing?

Tennis

5 Who gave his name to a system of printing that used raised dots to help the blind to read?

Louis Braille

It's a fact! Scientists are working on using sharks as spies. They will implant electrodes in the sharks' brains so they can control them remotely. The sharks could be used to track sea vessels.

Picture Clue
Quiz 72
Question 2

6 What is a shrine – a robe that is used to dress a dead person or a sacred place?

A sacred place

7 Is Jacqueline Wilson a famous author or a Hollywood actress?

A famous author

8 What S is a person who passes on national secrets to other countries?

Spy

9 Who goes to kindergarten – young children or elderly people?

Young children

10 Which type of car racing are Jenson Button and Lewis Hamilton famous for?

Formula One (F1)

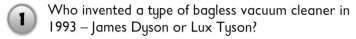

Quiz 72 • How We Live

QUESTIONS

ANSWERS

1 Who invented a type of bagless vacuum cleaner in 1993 – James Dyson or Lux Tyson?

James Dyson

2 What number do many people consider to be unlucky?

13

3 Who might use sleight-of-hand in their job – a butcher or a magician?

A magician

4 Which cricket team won the Ashes in 2005 – the first time they had won it since the 1980s?

England

5 Are dungarees trousers or shoes?

Trousers

It's a fact! The Ashes is a test cricket series that has been played by old rivals England and Australia for more than 100 years. The small trophy contains the ashes of a bail – part of a cricket stump.

Picture Clue
Quiz 71
Question 2

6 Which Children's Laureate is especially famous for his pictures of gorillas?

Anthony Browne

7 In 1997 Elton John sang *Candle in the Wind* at the funeral of which princess?

Princess Diana

8 Which language is most common in the world – Arabic or English?

English

9 What kind of prehistoric animal was *Tyrannosaurus rex*?

A dinosaur

10 Where was the record-breaking sprinter Usain Bolt born?

Jamaica

1 Which invaders did Queen Boudicca and her troops fight against – the Vikings or the Romans?

The Romans

2 Are people who use both hands equally well called ambidextrous or bi-handed?

Ambidextrous

3 What type of scientist studies rocks?

Geologist

4 If a woman is described as 'expectant', what condition is she in?

Pregnant

5 In what year did South Africans vote for Nelson Mandela to become their president – 1944 or 1994?

1994

It's a fact! The samurai were Japanese warriors from the 8th to the 19th century. They fought with long curved swords called katanas, and followed a warrior way of life called Bushido.

Picture Clue
Quiz 74
Question 8

6 Whose face appears on all British banknotes?

The Queen's

7 Which saint converted the Irish people to Christianity about 1500 years ago?

Saint Patrick

8 What is the top job that has been held by Gordon Brown, Tony Blair and Margaret Thatcher?

Prime Minister

9 If someone can sing high notes are they called a bass or a soprano?

A soprano

10 What country did samurai warriors come from?

Japan

Quiz 74 • How We Live

1 What does a zoologist study?

Animals

2 Which pop star sang the song 'Poker Face'?

Lady Gaga

3 According to legend, Isaac Newton discovered gravity as he saw which type of fruit fall from a tree?

An apple

4 Which city is known as the Big Apple?

New York

5 On what part of your body would you wear a balaclava?

Head

It's a fact! Sir Isaac Newton (1643–1727) is regarded as one of the most important scientists to have ever lived. He developed ideas about maths, light, colour and forces, including gravity.

Picture Clue
Quiz 73
Question 1

6 Is Paula Radcliffe famous for running marathons or throwing the javelin?

Running marathons

7 What does an architect do – design buildings or study the history of humans?

Design buildings

8 What type of shelter do Inuit people build from blocks of ice?

Igloo

9 What S is a person's last or family name?

Surname

10 Which European country has the biggest population – Russia or Germany?

Russia

QUESTIONS

ANSWERS

1 Rebecca Adlington is an Olympic athlete. What is her sport?

Swimming

2 What is the name of the Jewish holy book?

Torah

3 What is the name of the Queen's eldest son?

Prince Charles

4 What do the initials UN stand for?

United Nations

5 What is another name for Norsemen?

Vikings

It's a fact! Rebecca Adlington won two Gold medals for the 400 metres and 800 metres freestyle swimming events at the Beijing Olympics in 2008.

Picture Clue
Quiz 76
Question 1

6 What side of the road do people drive on in the USA?

The right

7 On which TV dance show have Alesha Dixon and Arlene Phillips worked as judges?

Strictly Come Dancing

8 When people move to a new country are they called immigrants or imminents?

Immigrants

9 Who is President of the United States of America?

Barack Obama

10 If someone wishes you 'bon anniversaire' in French, what special day are you celebrating?

Your birthday

1 In the 19th century, which group of brave warriors from southern Africa fought against the British?

The Zulu

2 Which football team would you associate with John Terry and Frank Lampard?

Chelsea

3 When someone talks rubbish, are they said to be talking gobbledegook or nincompoop?

Gobbledegook

4 Was Pocahontas a Native American princess or the daughter of a French Emperor?

A Native American princess

5 If someone performs a task 'solo' are they doing it alone or as part of a team?

Alone

It's a fact! A wedding is a ceremony in which two people are united in marriage. There are different customs around the world, and many involve the offering of rings.

Picture Clue
Quiz 75
Question 5

6 What protective garment stops your clothes from getting messy when you cook?

Apron

7 A woman who is getting married is called a bride. What name is given to the man she is marrying?

Bridegroom, or groom

8 In what type of building do Hindus worship?

Temple

9 Do identical twins have identical fingerprints?

No

10 What word begining with A do magicians use when they perform a magic trick?

Abracadabra

Quiz 77 • How We Live

QUESTIONS

ANSWERS

1 What did medieval knights use to clean their wounds – oil or vinegar?

Vinegar

2 What red paper flower do people wear on Remembrance Day?

Poppy

3 In 1930, Amy Johnson became the first woman to fly a plane alone from Britain to which country?

Australia

4 Which secret assassins from Japan were skilled in martial arts?

Ninjas

5 What would you call your mother's sister's son – cousin or uncle?

Cousin

It's a fact! On Remembrance Day, 11th November, people wear poppies to remember those who died fighting in wars. This tradition began after the First World War, which ended on 11th November 1918.

Picture Clue
Quiz 78
Question 3

6 What number do most superstitious people believe is lucky?

Seven

7 If you train for dressage, show jumping and eventing what is your sport?

Horse riding

8 What name is given to a swimsuit for girls and women that has two separate parts?

Bikini

9 What day is also known as April Fool's Day?

1st April

10 What style of music was Bob Marley famous for?

Reggae

Quiz 78 • How We Live

1 Who invented the television – John Logie Baird or Thomas Edison?

John Logie Baird

2 Which fizzy drink was invented by Doctor Pepper?

Dr Pepper

3 Which type of warriors fought in ancient Roman amphitheatres?

Gladiators

4 What name beginning with J was the most popular for baby boys born in the UK in 2008?

Jack

5 Who flew the Jolly Roger flag from their ships?

Pirates

It's a fact! John Logie Baird (1888–1946) was a Scottish engineer who invented the television in the 1920s. The BBC broadcast the world's first television programmes in 1936.

Picture Clue
Quiz 77
Question 4

6 What currency do Spanish people use – pounds, dollars or euros?

Euros

7 How many people play in a netball team – seven or 14?

Seven

8 What type of trousers did Levi Strauss help to invent?

Jeans

9 What sport do Jonny Wilkinson and Gavin Henson play?

Rugby

10 What are unmarried men sometimes called – bachelors or badgers?

Bachelors

Quiz 79 • How We Live

Who Invented What?

See if you can match the invention to the inventor.
The inventors' names might give you a clue.

Adolphe Sax, Alexander Graham Bell, Clarence Birdseye,
Erno Rubik, Gabriel Fahrenheit, Gottlieb Daimler,
John Boyd Dunlop, Keith Kellogg, Laszlo Biro, Levi Strauss.

1 Telephone

2 Breakfast cereal

3 Thermometer

7 Frozen food

4 Ballpoint pen

5 Daimler car

6 Tyre

8 Jeans

9 Rubik's cube

10 Saxophone

Quiz 80 • How We Live

Sporting Heroes

Can you match the famous sports people to
the close-up pictures of the sport they play?

Amir Khan, Cristiano Ronaldo, Jonny Wilkinson,
Kevin Pietersen, Lewis Hamilton, Paula Radcliffe,
Rebecca Adlington, Serena Williams, Tiger Woods, Usain Bolt.

Quiz 81 • True or False

1 Some plants eat animals.

True

2 Children in China have to learn thousands of characters when they learn to read and write.

True

3 The Atlantic Ocean is the largest ocean in the world.

False. The Pacific is the largest

4 The lead in a pencil is made from the same substance as diamonds.

True. Both are made of carbon

5 Tomatoes and red peppers are fruits.

True

It's a fact! Meat-eating plants, such as pitcher plants and venus fly traps, attract flies and other small animals to them. The animals become trapped and the plants produce juices to digest them.

Picture Clue
Quiz 82
Question 1

6 Babies and teenagers need more sleep than adults.

True

7 Strangler figs are jungle plants that wrap around a sleeping person's throat and strangle them.

False. These plants grow around trees

8 The words 'under,' 'before' and 'beneath' are all verbs.

False. They are prepositions

9 Scandanavia is part of Europe.

True

10 Wall•E is a Disney Pixar movie that was set in the future.

True. It was set in 2805

Quiz 82 • True or False

1 Your heart is also called a cardiac muscle.

True

2 There have been eight King Henrys in England but only two King Charleses.

True

3 Clarence Birdseye discovered a way to quickly freeze food in 1926.

True

4 Micky Wave invented the microwave oven.

False. It was invented by Dr Percy Spencer

5 Leotards are named after a French acrobat.

True. They are named after Jules Léotard

It's a fact! King Charles I (1600–1649) believed that kings got their power directly from God and could not be removed from the throne. He was proved wrong when he was captured and executed!

Picture Clue
Quiz 81
Question 7

6 The word 'already' has two Ls.

False. It has one

7 A capital letter A has two lines of symmetry.

False. It has one

8 Oil is put into engines to reduce friction and help the parts move smoothly.

True

9 There are three noughts in the figure fifty thousand.

False. There are four

10 The term 'cul-de-sac', which means a dead-end street, comes from the French for 'the bum of a bag'!

True

Quiz 83 • True or False

1 An extreme fear of something is called a rage.

False. Extreme fears are called phobias

2 About 50 people are attacked by sharks every year, but only one of those is likely to die.

True

3 The rafflesia flower smells of rotting meat.

True

4 Ancient Greeks believed that after death everyone went to a place called Hades.

True

5 Your smallest bone is in your little toe.

False. It is in your ear

It's a fact! There are five species of rhino – three live in Asia and two in Africa. Rhinos are often killed for their horns, because some people believe they have magical properties.

Picture Clue
Quiz 84
Question 10

6 The size of a computer's memory is measured in Bytes, Megabytes, Gigabytes and Terrabytes.

True

7 White rhinos are white.

False. They are actually grey

8 The Amazon rainforest is spreading.

False. It's shrinking as people cut down trees

9 66 divided by 11 is 6.

True

10 US presidents must be less than 50 years old.

False. President Reagan was 77

Quiz 84 • True or False

QUESTIONS

ANSWERS

1 Newspaper journalists normally write non-fiction.

True. Although they do make things up too

2 Roald Dahl wrote *James and the Giant Pineapple*.

False. He wrote *James and the Giant Peach*

3 *X-Factor* judge Cheryl Cole first found fame on a TV talent contest.

True. She took part in *Popstars: The Rivals*

4 In the 1980s, singer Michael Jackson had a hit single called 'Billie Jean'.

True

5 One in every 100 people is left-handed.

False. About one in ten is left-handed

It's a fact! Dogs are intelligent animals, which is why they can be trained to work with people. Rescue dogs are taught how to find victims trapped in rubble after earthquakes.

Picture Clue

QUIZ 83
Question 3

6 There are more people alive today than have ever lived.

True

7 The human brain can't feel pain.

True. It tells you if other body parts hurt

8 Most dogs can learn to understand at least 100 words.

True

9 A bibliophobe is a person who is scared of books.

True

10 A clarinet is like a violin, only bigger.

False. A clarinet is a wind instrument

Quiz 85 • True or False

QUESTIONS

ANSWERS

1 Marge Simpson has brown hair.

False. She has blue hair

2 All plants have green leaves.

False. They can be many colours

3 The Wimbledon tennis championship was first broadcast on BBC Television in 1937.

True

4 Lots of gases are invisible.

True

5 Goth, Creep and Punk are all types of music.

False. Creep is not a type of music

It's a fact! Vampires are mythical creatures that feed on the blood of humans. The myth may be based on vampire bats, which drink the blood of cows and other animals.

Picture Clue
Quiz 86
Question 1

6 9 x 120 is more than 1000.

True. It is 1080

7 Vampires were wiped out in the 19th century.

False. They never existed

8 A circle has no lines of symmetry.

False. It has an unlimited number

9 Barack Obama is the first African American to be president of the USA.

True

10 Proper nouns should always be written with a capital letter at the beginning.

True

Quiz 86 • True or False

QUESTIONS

ANSWERS

1 Butterflies are mostly active during the day, and moths are mostly nocturnal.

True

2 The prefix 'tri' at the beginning of a word means 'two'.

False. It means 'three', 'bi' means 'two'

3 Human nails are made of living cells.

False. Hair and nails are not alive

4 It takes 365¼ days for the Earth to orbit the Moon.

False. The Earth orbits the Sun, not the Moon

5 Ice melts at 0°C.

True

It's a fact! Cutting your nails or having a haircut doesn't hurt because hair and nails are not living. They are made from a protein called keratin – feathers contain keratin too!

Picture Clue

QUIZ 85
Question 9

6 The capital of the African country Burkina Faso is Ouagadougou.

True

7 The Pyrenees Mountains are where Canada and the USA meet.

False. They are where Spain and France meet

8 A lump of granite rock will dissolve if you leave it in milk for a few days.

False

9 England last won the football World Cup in 1999.

False. It was 1966

10 The word 'it' is a pronoun.

True

Quiz 87 • True or False

1 Aluminium is used to make planes because it is very strong but lightweight.

True

2 Carrots grow on trees.

False. They grow underground

3 Most house dust is dead skin cells and the remains of tiny animals that eat them.

True

4 The Sahara desert is in Australia.

False. It is in Africa

5 Water can reflect light.

True

It's a fact! House dust mites feed on dead skin and other dead body material. The mites are harmless, but their poo can make people sneeze, cough or suffer other allergic reactions.

Picture Clue
Quiz 88
Question 3

6 The box jellyfish is so deadly you are unlikely to live if you are stung.

True

7 Rockets travel faster than the speed of light.

False

8 Belgium is in France.

False. Belgium is a separate country

9 It's possible to turn the Sun's rays into electricity.

True. It is solar energy

10 Troy and Gabriella are characters from *High School Musical*.

True

Quiz 88 • True or False

QUESTIONS

ANSWERS

1 Seals and sea lions have whiskers.

True

2 Risotto is a type of pasta.

False. It is a rice dish

3 Flying fish grow wings and can fly for several kilometres at a time.

False. They glide over water using large fins

4 Lava from volcanoes can reach a sizzling 1200°C.

True

5 Printed margins are horizontal lines.

False. They are vertical lines

It's a fact! The way water goes down a plughole has nothing to do with geography. It is all to do with the shape of the basin and how the water is flowing already.

Picture Clue
Quiz 87
Question 10

6 Water goes down a plughole clockwise in Britain, but anti-clockwise in Australia.

False

7 Bactrian camels have two humps but dromedaries have one.

True

8 When people reach the North Pole, their blood is affected by the strong magnetic pull.

False

9 Edam, Brie and Feta were all in the Top 100 of girls' names in 1997.

False. They are types of cheese!

10 Junior Wilderness Explorer Russell is a character in the movie *Monsters Inc.*

False. He is a character in *Up*

Quiz 89 • True or False

Name the Dinosaurs

Each dinosaur has been given two
names. Which names are the true ones?

1 Velociraptor or
Vegasraptor

2 Trinnysaurus rox or
Tyrannosaurus rex

3 Allosaurus or
Allanosaurus

4 Hairosaurus or
Herrerasaurus

5 Stigosaurus or
Stegosaurus

6 Euoplocephalus or
Youplocephaus

7 Triceratops or
Trickeratops

8 Parasolosaurus or
Parasaurolophus

9 Brickiosaurus or
Brachiosaurus

10 Compsognathus or
Campsognathus

Quiz 90 • True or False

Extinct Animals

Look at these animals. They are all
extinct – true or false?

1 Giant anteater

2 Dodo

3 Giant panda

4 Mammoth

5 Hyaena

6 Giant elk

7 Polar bear

8 Ruffed lemur

9 Sabre-tooth cat

10 Red panda

Quiz 41 • Lucky Dip

1 What is the yellow part of an egg called?

Yolk

2 What are the two halves of the Earth called — hemispheres or semi-globes?

Hemispheres

3 How many lines of symmetry does a trapezium have?

One

4 Which planet is famous for its rings, Jupiter or Saturn?

Saturn

5 A CD is a compact disc. What is a DVD?

A digital versatile disc

It's a fact! Toy Story was the first ever fully computer-generated full-length movie. It took 27 animators and about 400 computer models to create the Toy Story characters.

Picture Clue
Quiz 42
Question 6

6 How many hours are in three days and nights?

72

7 Spell 'horizon'.

Horizon

8 What is five-tenths as a decimal?

0.5

9 What is the name of the nasty toy-torturing boy in Toy Story?

Sid (Phillips)

10 What do cooks use to fry food — water or oil?

Oil

Quiz 92 • Lucky Dip

QUESTIONS

ANSWERS

1 What B is a wireless system for sending data over short distances – Bluetooth or Blingtone?

Bluetooth

2 How many centimetres are in one kilometre?

100,000

3 What is electronic mail better known as?

Email

4 Does a 3D shape have three dimensions or three divisions?

Three dimensions

5 Would you use an 'A to Z' to find a street or the spelling of a word?

To find a street

It's a fact! At Halloween, faces are cut into pumpkins. When lit candles are put inside, the pumpkin face looks ghoulish. In the USA carved pumpkins are called Jack o' Lanterns.

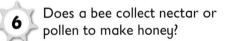

Picture Clue

Quiz 91
Question 4

6 Does a bee collect nectar or pollen to make honey?

Nectar

7 How many months are in three years?

36

8 What D is a collection of data with an index, which can be created with a computer?

Database

9 If you stop oxygen from reaching a fire, will it burn stronger or go out?

It will go out

10 Which festival is celebrated with pumpkins and dressing-up as witches, ghosts and skeletons?

Halloween

Quiz 93 • Lucky Dip

1 Beagles, retrievers, terriers and poodle are all types of what?

Dog

2 Does wool come from sheep or cows?

Sheep

3 What colour is Tinky Winky the Teletubby?

Purple

4 How many sides does a quadrilateral have?

Four

5 What L is a device that concentrates light waves into a very strong beam?

Laser

It's a fact! It is very unlikely that dinosaurs could swim but many giant marine reptiles were alive at the same time. Ichthyosaurus, for example, grew to 2 metres long and gave birth to live young.

Picture Clue

Quiz 94
Question 8

6 Does a sundial measure time or the size of moving planets?

Time

7 Could dinosaurs swim?

No

8 What is the next number in this sequence – 28, 35, 42, 49 …?

56

9 Limericks, haikus, ballads, sonnets and odes are all types of what?

Poem

10 How many seconds are in five minutes?

300

Quiz 94 • Lucky Dip

1 Is the Mediterranean a sea or an ocean?

A sea

2 How many minutes are in a quarter of an hour?

15

3 Web pages have their own unique address. Is this known as an HGV or a URL?

URL

4 Spell 'bicycle'.

Bicycle

5 Does rubber come from trees or rocks?

Trees

It's a fact! Rubber is a natural material that is produced by some trees. When the bark of the trees is cut, a thick white substance, called latex, leaks out and this is turned into rubber.

Picture Clue
Quiz 43
Question 2

6 What C is a maths instrument you would use to draw circles?

Compass

7 In which animated movie do the characters of Remy and Linguine appear?

Ratatouille

8 What A is a snowfall down a mountainside?

Avalanche

9 How many faces does a cube have?

Six

10 What is the fourth last letter of the alphabet?

W

Quiz 95 • Lucky Dip

1 Olive, sage and lime are all shades of which colour?

Green

2 What sea lies between Great Britain and Ireland?

The Irish Sea

3 What is 75 percent of 1000?

750

4 Perch, haddock, bream and cod are all types of what?

Fish

5 Which movie is named after the rubbish-collecting robot, Waste Allocation Load Lifter: Earth Class?

Wall•E

It's a fact! Rome was a Republic, ruled by a Senate rather than one person – until Julius Caesar decided he wanted to be King. Rome was ruled by Emperors for the next 500 years.

Picture Clue
QUIZ 96
Question 7

6 A TV programme begins at 6.35 p.m. and finishes at 7.10 p.m. How long is it?

35 minutes

7 Is leather a natural material or a synthetic one?

Natural

8 How many right angles are in a right-angled triangle?

One

9 What S is a piece of electronic equipment you might use to copy a printed picture onto a computer?

Scanner

10 Were Nero, Constantine, Hadrian, Trajan and Julius Caesar Roman emperors or Anglo-Saxon rulers?

Roman emperors

Quiz 96 • Lucky Dip

QUESTIONS

ANSWERS

1 When paper gets very hot does it melt or burn?

It burns

2 What colour is produced by mixing green and red paints together?

Brown

3 Does cotton come from a plant or an animal?

A plant

4 What P is the country where the city of Lisbon is found?

Portugal

5 Which ancient people staged gladiator fights – Arabs or Romans?

Romans

It's a fact! Diamonds are weighed in carats and each carat is equivalent to 200 milligrams, or 0.2 grams. The Star of Africa is a massive diamond in the Crown Jewels and it measures 530.2 carats.

Picture Clue

Quiz 95
Question 4

6 Which travelling Time Lord appears in TV's *Sarah Jane Adventures*?

Doctor Who

7 What F contains gunpowder and goes bang in the sky?

Fireworks

8 What shape is the base of a cone?

A circle

9 What E is the mixture of polluting gases that a car engine produces?

Exhaust

Is the size of a diamond measured in carats or turnips?

Carats

1 What is 50% of 200?

100

2 Is crimson a shade of red or green?

Red

3 What F are Fimbo, Florrie and Baby Pom?

Fimbles

4 Is the water in a river salty or fresh?

Fresh

5 What does a geologist study – rocks or the weather?

Rocks

It's a fact! Pasta is made from a dough of flour and water (and sometimes egg). The dough can be moulded into lots of different shapes, which is why there are more than 600 varieties of pasta!

Picture Clue

Quiz 48
Question 2

6 Where in your body would you find a drum?

In your ear

7 What does the 'I' stand for in ICT?

Information

8 When were the first electronic computers made, the 1940s or the 1970s?

The 1940s

9 If something has ignited, has it caught fire or melted?

Caught fire

10 Macaroni, penne and spaghetti are all types of what?

Pasta

10

Quiz 98 • Lucky Dip

1 What I is a network that connects millions of computers around the world?

Internet

2 What is the main ingredient of meringues – egg white or brown sugar?

Egg white

3 What A is a counting tool that has beads or counters on a frame of wires or rods?

Abacus

4 Are snakes slimy or smooth to touch?

Smooth

5 Is the Sun a planet or a star?

A star

It's a fact! Reptiles, such as snakes and lizards, have scaly skin. Most snakes have smooth, dry skin that helps them to slither, and prevents them losing water from their bodies.

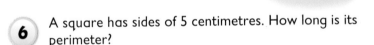

Picture Clue
Quiz 97
Question 6

6 A square has sides of 5 centimetres. How long is its perimeter?

20 centimetres

7 Iron, silver, gold and copper are all types of what?

Metal

8 Are three babies born at the same time are called triplets or trebles?

Triplets

9 What R is the distance between the centre of a circle and its edge?

Radius

10 In what parts of your body would you find an iris, a pupil and a lens?

Eyes

Feeling those Emoticons

Emoticons are used in text messages
to give them extra meaning or expression.

Can you work out the meaning of
the emoticons below?

Quiz 100 • Lucky Dip

In the Mood for Fruit

Tropical fruits are tasty and are used in desserts or eaten on their own.

Can you name each tropical fruit?

1

2

3

4

5

6

7

8

9

10

ANSWERS 1. Kiwi 2. Grapefruit 3. Apricot 4. Star fruit 5. Fig 6. Coconut 7. Papaya 8. Mango 9. Lime 10. Pineapple

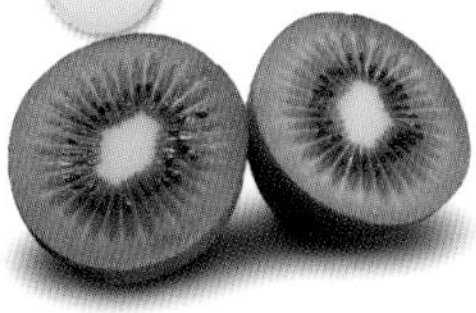

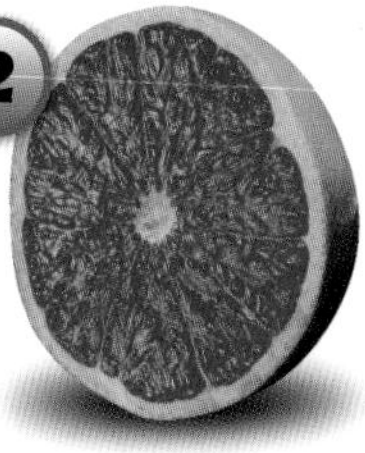

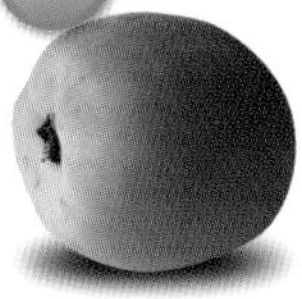

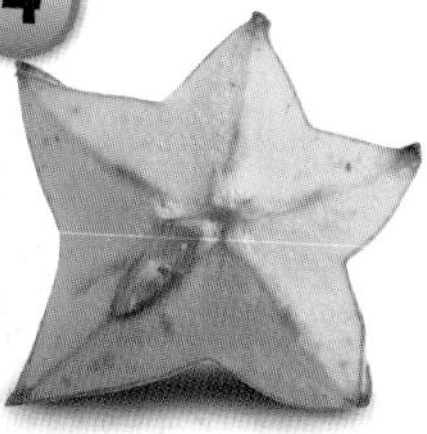

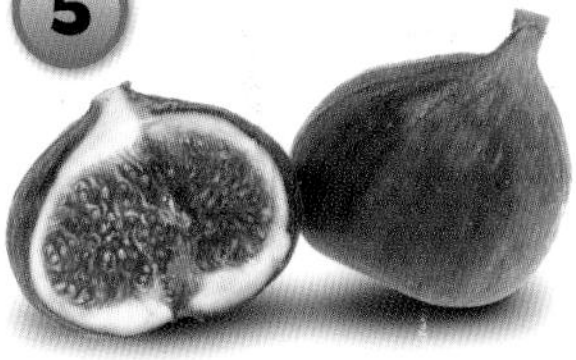

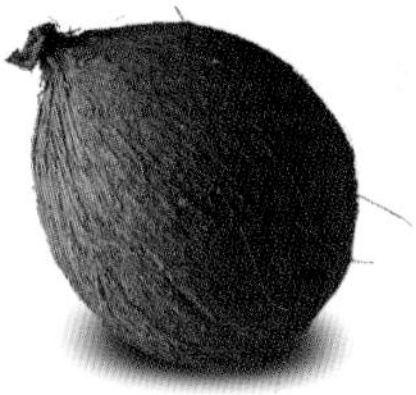

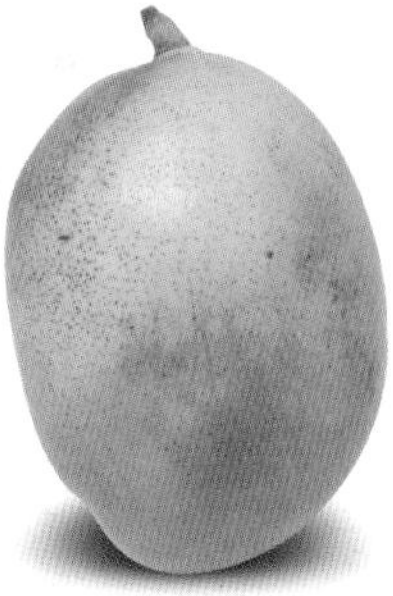

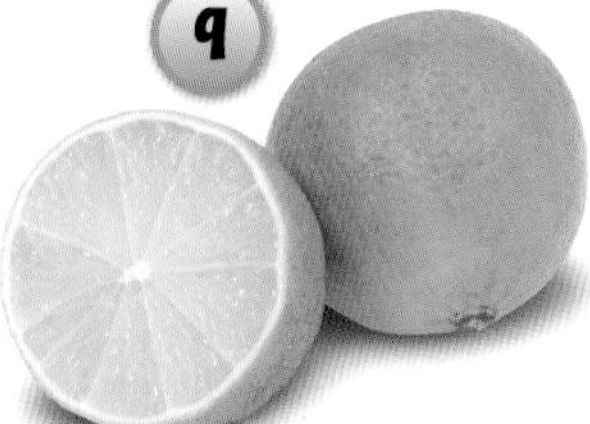

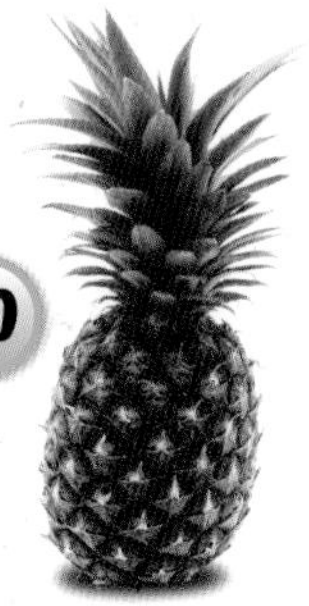

SCORECARDS

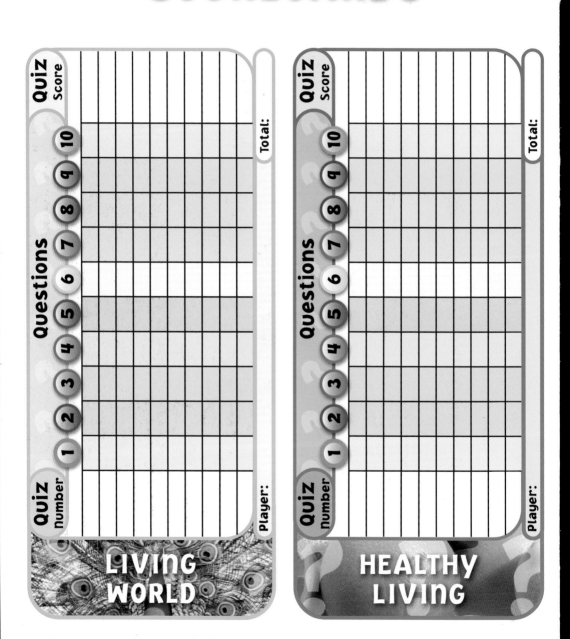

LIVING WORLD

Quiz number | Questions: 1 2 3 4 5 6 7 8 9 10 | Quiz Score

Player: | Total:

HEALTHY LIVING

Quiz number | Questions: 1 2 3 4 5 6 7 8 9 10 | Quiz Score

Player: | Total:

Photocopy the scorecards instead of writing in the book, so you can play again and again. Don't forget – for each section, you'll need one scorecard for each player. See pages 6–7 for help on how to play.

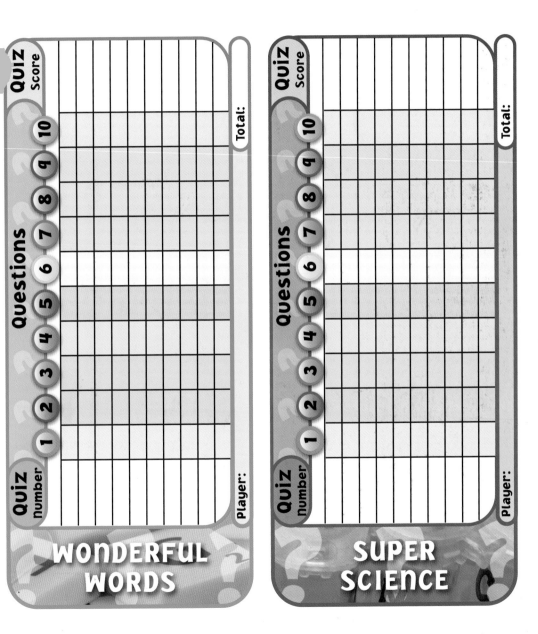

Quiz number | **Questions** 1 2 3 4 5 6 7 8 9 10 | **Quiz Score** | Total: | Player:

WONDERFUL WORDS

Quiz number | **Questions** 1 2 3 4 5 6 7 8 9 10 | **Quiz Score** | Total: | Player:

SUPER SCIENCE

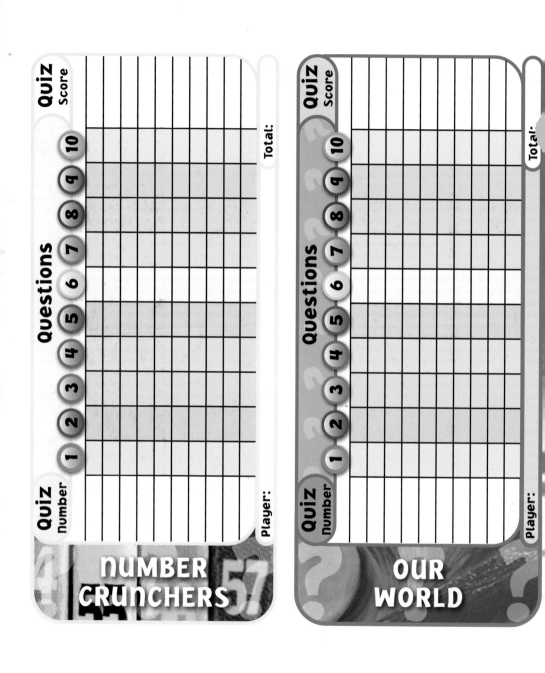

Quiz number

Questions
1 2 3 4 5 6 7 8 9 10

Quiz Score

Total:

Player:

NUMBER CRUNCHERS

Quiz number

Questions
1 2 3 4 5 6 7 8 9 10

Quiz Score

Total:

Player:

OUR WORLD

PAST TIMES

Quiz number	Questions										Quiz Score
	1	2	3	4	5	6	7	8	9	10	

Player: Total:

HOW WE LIVE

Quiz number	Questions										Quiz Score
	1	2	3	4	5	6	7	8	9	10	

Player: Total:

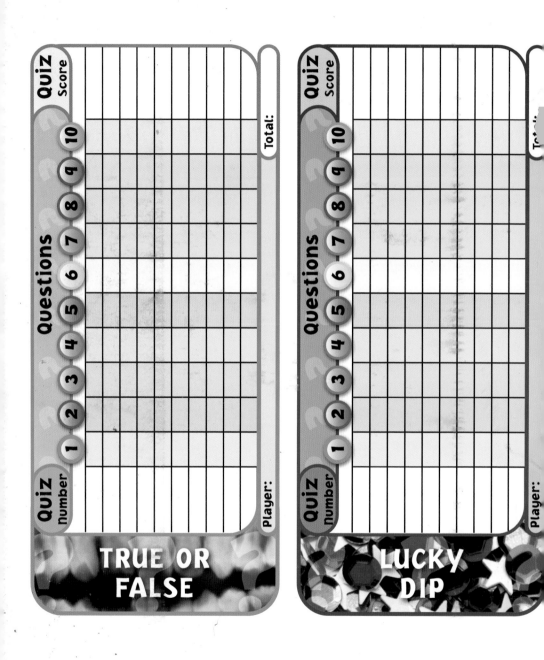

TRUE OR FALSE

Quiz Number	Questions 1	2	3	4	5	6	7	8	9	10	Quiz Score

Player: Total:

LUCKY DIP

Quiz Number	Questions 1	2	3	4	5	6	7	8	9	10	Quiz Score

Player: Total: